THE WRONG SIDE OF THE TRACK

FRED JENNINGS AND TRISH JENNINGS

© Trish Jennings & Noodle Books (Kevin Robertson) 2012

ISBN 978-1-906419-19-6

First published in 2012

Produced by Noodle Books (Kevin Robertson) on behalf of Trish Jennings - publisher.

NOODLE BOOKS PO Box 279, Corhampton, SOUTHAMPTON. SO32 3ZX

www.noodlebooks.co.uk

Printed in England by Ian Allan Printing.

Front cover / title page - *Fred and Cliff Jennings. Their mother Mabel wrote on the back 'Gussie (as in Gorgeous?) and Cliffie, June 1914', making Ashcott the most likely location. 'Gussie' was five years and ten months and 'Cliffie' was four years and one month.*

ACKNOWLEDGEMENTS

So many people have been involved in the preparation of this book it would be impossible to mention them all individually. There are a few whose contributions I must acknowledge because without them it would never have happened:

Gill and Michael Callister, my sister and brother-in-law, who did so much of the research. Gill not only assisted in the editing of our Dad's memoir but also acted as proof-reader.

Philip Hocking, the researcher at the Somerset Record Office, who was always there to answer my many queries and requests for various documents.

John Jennings, archivist for the Stratford & Midland Junction Railway, who carried out extensive research on my behalf into the Fenny Compton site.

Kevin Robertson, for agreeing to produce this book and for encouraging me to complete the task at times of self-doubt, and there were many.

Thanks also go to: Nick Fear (for the research at Kew), Janet Hubert, Brian Hutchings, Sonia Smith, Ann Tonkins, Mary Willcocks and the staff of the following organisations:

The County Record Offices of Somerset, Warwickshire and Devon,
Somerset Studies Library,
Somerset Rural Life Museum (David Walker),
South Gloucestershire Library Information Service,
Libraries in Bridgwater, Stratford-upon-Avon, Winterbourne (my local) and Bristol Reference Library
Land Registry.

Although every effort has been made to ensure the accuracy of the contents of Parts I and II, the responsibility for any errors and omissions lies with me and I am very sorry if anyone has been misled, misinformed or misquoted.

THE *WRONG* SIDE OF THE TRACK

The journey in this book begins and ends in Somerset, focusing on the lives of four generations of men, from my father to my great-great-grandfather. It spans more than two centuries, centuries which witnessed some of the greatest upheavals and changes that ever took place in this country, brought about by the Industrial Revolution and the two world wars. Set against the history of mankind, this is a relatively short time, but the progress made in so many areas was phenomenal and surely unprecedented in any previous age.

The incentive for the book has its origins in the tales my father, Frederick Charles Jennings, used to relate about his childhood, which was spent during the early part of the twentieth century in the neighbouring villages of Ashcott and Shapwick. It occurred to me that his was a way of life which had clearly gone forever: the arrival of the petrol engine and modern technology put an end to what now seems to us an almost feudal existence. I mentioned to my dad that he ought to record his memories of that bygone era, and I'm pleased to say that he was very willing to do so, as it was the finest legacy he could have left.

When he asked me what to include in his memoir, I suggested that he wrote about everything he could remember, right up until the time he left Shapwick in 1930. That is exactly what he did, sitting in his garden shed, bashing away on an ancient typewriter. He started writing in the 1970s, but it wasn't until a year or so after his death in 2003 that I decided to read it. I actually found it comforting because I could almost hear him saying the words in his own inimitable style. It felt as though I was starting out on a journey, discovering along the way so much that I didn't know about my dad and what had shaped his life and character. Most of all, I was amazed by the wealth of detail he was able to recall, which influenced my decision to publish it. The thought that all the effort he had put into it might be wasted and end up in the bin on my demise appalled me.

My father would never have claimed to be a writer, so 'Cider with Rosie' it ain't, but it is a valuable collection of boyhood-into-adulthood memories, worth preserving for future generations to enjoy. I'm not sure what his reaction to this book would have been, but I hope and suspect that he would have been quite pleased. Around the time he was writing, he took so many photographs of the places featured in his story that I assume they were intended to illustrate it. The fact that the prints and transparencies were carefully annotated adds weight to this assumption and I've used some of the captions provided by my dad. As many of the buildings have been altered or demolished, the photos may be of historical interest to local people in years to come.

Before publication could take place, some reorganisation of the material was necessary, and for that I enlisted the help of my sister, Gill. It looked as though Dad had started to try and write the memoir in chronological order, but this had presented difficulties. For instance, childhood memories are notoriously random and so it wasn't an easy task to produce a connected and coherent account. He then changed tack and began writing about individual, diverse topics, such as cider-making, Bridgwater Fair, the pheasant shoot and bell-ringing, to name but a few. Gill and I have tried to arrange the content according to specific subjects, each with a main heading, then with sub-headings as and when appropriate. Whether we have got it right, only Dad could say, which makes me wish I had set about it while he was still here. Apart from some further minor editing to avoid repetition and maintain continuity, the account is essentially in my dad's own words, and those who knew him will recognise that.

Although he went into great detail when writing about the things which interested him, there are gaps, and I regret not asking him to describe how domestic chores, such as the cooking and laundry, were carried out and how their homes were illuminated and heated. He did say that he could remember electricity being installed in Shapwick, during the 1920s he thought. Until then, presumably, candles or gas and oil lamps provided artificial light, and ranges and open fires heated the houses. I imagine he considered such issues to be the concern of the womenfolk and he concentrated on more manly occupations. His recall of contemporary farm machinery is so detailed that, in places, it almost resembles an instruction manual, useful if you're looking to recreate haymaking 1920s' style. (If the world's supply of oil runs out, then it may well become a reality.)

There are some amusing anecdotes about a few of the villagers, including a man who made quite an impression on my dad and went on to become a celebrated garden designer. His touching portrayal of some of the poorest inhabitants is very moving - they suffered the kind of grinding poverty, alien to us today, with equanimity and resignation. The daily life of the village is well documented, revealing the kind of community spirit that can only exist amongst a small population, all known to each other, unlike the anonymity of modern towns and cities. Most striking is the freedom of my father's childhood; he was able to roam and play in the countryside, unencumbered by the dangers facing today's children. Of course there were tragedies, and Dad had a few narrow escapes himself. It is clear to me that his encounters and experiences in the small Somerset village of Shapwick largely moulded the wonderful, philosophical man he was to become. Here, then, in part one, are the reminiscences of a very practical, pragmatic and down-to-earth person, who had a lifelong, insatiable curiosity about how things worked.

Trish Jennings

Bristol 2012

Brian Hutchings

'As a historian, I have always regarded memoirs as source material. A memoir provides a record not so much of the memoirist as of the memoirist's world.'

(From 'Memoirs of a Geisha' by Arthur Golden, Vintage, 1998)

FRED'S MEMOIR:

IN THE BEGINNING

I was born on 6th August 1908 at 2 Oldfield Road, Stoke Newington, London, the home of my mother's sister, Rose Willcocks. My father was at that time a constable in the Metropolitan Police, stationed at Cannon's Row, near the Houses of Parliament.

STOKE NEWINGTON: No. 2 Oldfield Road circa 1978.

Some six weeks after my birth, Dad left the police to become the landlord at the Albion Inn, Ashcott, about six miles from my mother's birthplace at Bawdrip, near Bridgwater. I cannot of course recall the early days at the Albion but certain things stick out in the memory up to the time we left in 1915. My brother Clifford was born there on 1st May 1910 and as he was the first child to be granted

this honour he was christened Clifford Albion. I used to think I could remember being lifted up to see him in bed with Mum but as I was only 21 months old I am no longer so sure. In about 1912 Mum gave birth to a stillborn boy who she used to say would have been named Arthur had he survived. He was buried in Ashcott Churchyard.

The Albion was situated on sloping ground, and there were three floors. The kitchen was on the lower one with the cellar adjoining. The bars were on the next floor, on the level with the main road where the entrance was. The top floor consisted of bedrooms. The licensing laws at that time allowed public houses to be open continuously all day long on weekdays; short of someone being behind the bar the whole time, it was necessary, at the sound of a call or whistle, for Mum or Dad to climb the stone stairs from the kitchen (living quarters) to the bar to deal with the customer. During the morning or afternoon this could mean serving one drink to one customer, more often than not a tramp, who would linger for an hour or so over two pennyworth of cider, which meant constant attendance behind the bar. As Dad was often out in the yard or orchard, attending to chickens and other livestock, the job of serving fell mostly on Mum. In later years she often used to relate what a burden it was running up and down that horrible, dark, stone stairway, especially with two small children to care for.

On Sunday afternoon it was usual for Mum and Dad to try and sleep in the kitchen chairs, and it was on one such occasion that I decided to try a drink of beer from one of the barrels in the cellar. I turned the tap on but couldn't turn it off after filling the cup. I had to wake Dad to come to the rescue and, as this took some little time, several pints must have escaped. As Dad never laid a hand on either of us I got off lighter than I deserved. I must have been about five. I had to fetch Dad on another occasion when I laid a turkey out with a stick because I thought it was going to attack me as it came gobbling towards me. It came round all right.

In 1913 I started school at Ashcott and the headmaster was Mr King. The school was about three-quarters of a mile away and I used to walk each way. I cannot remember about the midday meal but it wasn't provided at school, so I think I must have taken sandwiches as I do recall the schoolbag.

One day I discovered I could whistle and upon getting home in the afternoon I whistled on entering the front door. Sure enough Mum came up the stairs as usual to serve the customer. She wasn't all that pleased at the time but used to laugh about it in later years.

After the start of the Great War in 1914, army lorries appeared on the roads and the white dust thrown up from the stone surface used to be most noticeable on the hedgerows. At this time the horse-drawn mail used to run from Street, or Glastonbury, to Bridgwater. It was a squarish, red, box-shaped affair on four wheels, drawn by one horse, with the driver sitting on top of the box. I think it was at about 5.30pm that the driver made his daily call for a drink, and this was the signal for Clifford and me to be put to bed, at least in the winter months.

Apart from walking our only means of transport was a pony and trap which Mum used to visit her parents at Bawdrip. Dad used to drive to market at Bridgwater on Wednesdays and Glastonbury which I think was on Thursdays. The pony was stabled at the Bull and Butcher pub in Bridgwater and at the Lamb in Glastonbury. There was a fishmonger in attendance at Glastonbury with whom Dad used to 'have a deal', as he termed it. If Mum asked for two or three bloaters he would arrive home with about

1. Luckily, the pony could find its way home unaided after stopping at the pub, and did so on at least one occasion. Some joker had turned its collar upside down and there was no sign of my grandfather. He was discovered by my grandmother, lying on the floor of the trap, in a drunken state. His fellow drinkers obviously had a sense of humour and chucked him aboard, then set the pony off home. Dad had forgotten, or preferred to omit, this episode as he told the tale – many times!

Right - ASHCOTT: The School, 1982.

Bottom - *ASHCOTT: School photograph, 1914. Fred is sixth from the left in the middle row.*

The 33 children pictured probably comprised the infants' department as none looks older than seven or eight.

a dozen as he said they were cheaper that way. As half or more would have gone bad before being consumed, Mum used to try and explain that those we had eaten cost a good deal more in the end than if he had bought the number she had asked for. I don't think she ever managed to curb his enthusiasm for 'having a deal'. On his way home from Bridgwater he used to call at the New Inn (now the Toby Inn) at Chilton Polden. This came to light by the fact that the pony used to try and pull up at the front door when

Mum was returning from Bawdrip.[1 opposite]

Dad had always been very athletic and he was 100 yards and high jump champion of the Metropolitan Police when he left in 1908. When he came to the Albion word got round that he could run a bit, prompted no doubt by the fact some of his trophies were on show to the customers. At this time Ernie Cox of Catcott was 100 yards champion of the Polden Hill sports held annually at Chilton Polden.

Stourhead, 1983.

He arrived at the pub one day with a challenge to Dad for a 100 yards race between them for a stake of one golden sovereign a side. The race duly took place, and Mum held the two sovereigns. She was left holding them at the end as Dad won quite easily. Up to the time I left Shapwick in 1930 Dad and Ernie Cox were the closest of friends but the Polden Hill sports meeting probably died out with the start of the 1914 war. Soon after I was stationed at Staple Hill in December 1949,[2] I had occasion to meet Mr Kidd, the headmaster of Page Park School, in connection with damage by some of the pupils. I had heard he came from Somerset, and it transpired his home was Westhay, next door to Shapwick. He attended Dr Morgan's School, as did I, but had left before I started. He asked me if my father kept the Albion and, upon hearing he did, he told me he had witnessed the race between Dad and Ernie Cox, and how surprised most spectators were by the result. Apart from Mum, I never met anyone else who was there. Mr Kidd also told me that the then vicar of Mangotsfield, the Rev Beard, was an ex-Dr Morgan's boy, and he later officiated at the funeral of the Rev W.E. Catlow, my old headmaster.

When war broke out in 1914 I went to stay with Mum's sister, Sophia, at Stourhead in Wiltshire. Her husband, Uncle Walter, was footman/chauffeur to Sir Henry Hoare

at the big house at Stourhead, now a well-known National Trust property. I can't remember how long my stay was but I was there long enough to have to go to school for a week or so. A boy who lived next door was named Willie Hollis and he used to play with a small four-wheeled trolley on the green opposite the house, which is still there near the Bristol High Cross. I used to be given rides in his trolley. Occasionally Uncle Walter would bring one of the cars and take Aunt Soph and me for a ride which was very exciting. It was an open touring car, possibly a Metallurgique, made in Belgium. Somewhere near Shaftsbury one of the acetylene headlamps fell off when we were in motion and was badly damaged. Uncle Walter took it to a nearby garage for repair. There was a fairly short, steep hill near home and once, when going up, the car just would not make it to the top. There we were running backwards down the hill with Uncle Walter frantically looking back and twisting the steering wheel until we came to a halt at the bottom. We eventually got over the top and, on looking back, I think it must have been by making the ascent in low gear all the way.

Once he took me to Stourhead House and put me in the back of one of the big saloon cars in the garage with the doors shut while he went about his business. The upholstery was Bedford cord, and there were straphangers

---

2. He had joined Gloucestershire Police in 1931.
3. A copy of the entry in the register, sent to my father by the school, confirms that he and Cliff started there together on 12th October 1914.

8

of the same material over each rear door to assist passengers getting in or out.

His parents lived at Kilmington, the next village near King Alfred's Tower, and he used to take me on the crossbar of his bicycle when visiting them. The journey took us through a park with gates at one or both ends, and it was my job to reach forward and unfasten the latch when passing through.

When I returned to the Albion I think I must have resumed school at Shapwick rather than at Ashcott, as Clifford and I were both attending Shapwick School before we left the Albion in 1915.[3 opposite] About this time I was presented with a pedal car, chain driven with fixed wheels, which I tried out by going down Pedwell Hill at the side of the Albion. That was my first lesson about the need for brakes, of which this car had none. I ended up in the hedge halfway down as I was quite unable to hold back with my feet on the pedals.

There were wide double gates which opened on to Pedwell Hill from the yard and these could be seen from the kitchen window. Someone was leading a bull which broke loose and I saw this enormous animal astride our gates, having evidently tried to jump over into the yard. The outcome I don't recollect as I think I ran upstairs for safety.

In the garden there was a well which was said to be 60 feet deep. This was our water supply. Once, Mum found Ada Stevens and me, lying on our tummies and looking down the well. We were both about five years old and were severely warned not to do that again.

On 4th January 1914 Mum's father, Frank March, died at his home at Bawdrip and I remember going with Mum in the pony and trap as soon as she got the news. Grandmother March was sitting huddled up in the corner of the living room, looking very dejected. He was only 64 years old and had suffered very badly from what was supposed to be rheumatism, as did many of the people who worked on the land in those days. Living in an old, stone-built, cold cottage as they did must have hastened his death. The cottage was later burned to the ground when Mum's brother Fred and his family occupied it. The fire was said officially, for insurance purposes, to have been caused by a jackdaw's nest catching fire in the chimney. There were other versions, somewhat nearer to the truth, I suspect. However, a new house arose from the insurance money, built by Uncles Fred and Jack who were regarded as being as good at their jobs, as carpenter and bricklayer respectively, as any in Somerset.

Uncle Walter was an army reservist, and I recall how he used to say he would be called up, which he was in

STOURHEAD: Bristol High Cross and the cottages, 1983.

Fred astride the Coventry Eagle bicycle in his Doctor Morgan's School uniform, accompanied by a mystery girlfriend.

November 1914. When he went into the army, Aunt Soph left Stourhead and came to live either with her mother at Bawdrip or at the Albion. She was certainly at the Albion on 24th June 1915, when my cousin Elsie was born, because I definitely remember her calling out when in labour a day or so before the birth, the significance of which I did not appreciate at the time.

It was probably around this time that I started riding a bicycle. One day I was at Grandma's at Bawdrip with Aunt Soph, and we had to get to the Albion. Aunt Soph had a bike, on which I think I must have already had a ride, as I set off first. After about a mile I left the bike against a gate to a field and then walked on. Aunt Soph had followed on foot and when she reached the bike she took over and eventually came riding past me. About a mile on she left the bike, and I took over when I came to it, and so on until we reached home. At this time I had to ride standing on the pedals as I was not nearly tall enough to sit on the seat. I didn't have a bike of my own until about 1918 when Dad bought Ken Wren's second-hand Coventry Eagle for £3.

Uncle Fred, the carpenter, was not called up during the war but was directed to work on building army huts. This took him to Salisbury Plain among other places. I don't know how he travelled home while on leave but I well remember that when he called at the Albion once, on his way home to Bawdrip, he was blind drunk. He got down on the floor of the kitchen and was being sick. Mum had got hold of his coat collar and was trying to get him to his feet. She was laughing her head off but, on looking back, I still can't understand what was so funny about it, especially with the clearing up which followed.

Some time in 1915 Mum saw a soldier in uniform walking past the Albion and, on enquiring, was told he

*This page - The March Grandparents. **Above:** Granny March as a young girl (On the back of the photo frame is written: Elizabeth West had her Portrate [sic] taken when she was 12 years of age in 1862). **Bottom, left to right -** Elizabeth and Frank March in 1906. Granny March in old age – she died on 16th October 1939, aged 89.*

11

BAWDRIP: The grave of Frank and Elizabeth March and of their son Tom (Frank was 66 and not 64 as Fred thought).

Cannibal Isle, And lived in some huts on bananas and nuts, Crying out Hari-Kazoo all the while!' And so on…. 'I'm in love with your sweet Irish smile, Sally O'Malley from Evergreen Alley was wrecked on a Cannibal Isle.'

Mill House Memories

After the start of the Great War in 1914, the heavy loss of life and the fact it was supposed to be over by Christmas 1914 but wasn't, meant that the call-up of civilians became necessary. Those in occupations that were not vital soon got their enlistment papers. Dad, born in 1876, was now 39 (mid 1915) and quite likely to have become a soldier if he remained at the Albion. Consequently, sometime before the end of 1915, we moved to the Mill House at Shapwick, and attached were the flourmill, a three-storey building, disused since the early part of the century, and some outhouses and a stable. I think there was also a small amount of land and, from this and his ability at general dealing, Dad somehow eked out a living.[4] He kept a few pigs and laying hens. He escaped being called up during the war but in any case he had a physical disability in one hip which caused him pain right through to the end of his life. He was very athletic while in the Metropolitan Police and, as previously stated, was actually the 100 yards and high jump champion sometime between 1903 and 1908. This was later to be blamed for his disability. After a medical examination many years later he was told that the hip joint had possibly been dislocated at some time or other. He became a special constable during the war but I never recall him doing any duty.

When we left the Albion, a Mr Saunders became the landlord and, following him, in 1919, it was taken over by Uncle Walter and Aunt Soph, so eventually cousin Elsie returned to her birthplace.

One Christmas I was sent to stay with Aunt Elsie and Uncle Tom at Uphill. The war was still on, and Aunt Soph was staying there at Uphill with her daughter Elsie. I think cousin Arthur, Aunt Elsie's first child, had been born but I am not sure. Presumably due to lack of accommodation, I had to sleep at the nearby home of Uncle Tom's parents. I was so homesick that Aunt Soph and Aunt Elsie walked me to Uphill Station and put me on the train for home after two nights at most. I don't know how Mum was told I had cut short my visit and can only think it was by telegram. I know that I wasn't all that popular with either aunt at the time. I remember arriving home and being most upset at seeing the presents Clifford had collected as I hadn't got any. I'm sure Mum remedied this.

was on leave from France and had walked from Bridgwater (nine miles). I think his name was Jeanes and he was heading for his home at Ashcott. Mum thought this was outrageous and she would have met him with the pony and trap at Bridgwater Station had she known. There was no public transport (by road) whatever then.

One day a phonograph appeared and was played but I can't remember the tune or the operator. It wasn't ours but I recall the records were cylindrical in shape and were slid over a horizontal roller-shaped arm of corresponding size. The sound box with needle was then applied as on the ordinary gramophones with the flat, circular records which came later. Aunt Soph had one of the latter which she kept at Bawdrip, and I am supposed to have completely dismantled the clockwork motor. I had got it all back together, except for one part, before being caught. Someone else had to finish the job but it still worked and I recall two of the records. One was 'In the Blue Ridge Mountains of Virginia', which was sung by Laurel and Hardy in a film many years later. The other was 'Sally O'Malley from Evergreen Alley was wrecked on a

4. Cliff recalled that, during the First World War, their father used to travel to London where he bought old street horses at auction. He took them back to Shapwick, presumably by train, where he sold them to the farmers whose horses had been requisitioned by the army.
5. My dad admitted that Cliff had acted on his instructions.

BAWDRIP: Uncle Fred's house, indicated, which arose, like the phoenix, from the ashes of the burnt-out cottage, 1975.

Clifford and I had each been given an airgun (King or Daisy make), which fired the usual slug pellets, as a Christmas present. We took our guns on a visit to Grandmother March at Bawdrip. On reaching the point where the living-room window looked out onto the road, Clifford announced our arrival by firing at it.[5 opposite] We never imagined this would shatter the glass in the way it did, and I don't think Grandma ever forgot it. Cousin Elsie, living there at the time with her mum, was sitting near the window and Grandma always insisted that she saw the slug pass over the top of Elsie's head. Her eyesight was good right up to the time of her death at nearly 90, but I think she overstretched it a bit in this case. Clifford got into plenty of trouble with Mum over this but that time his gun wasn't confiscated. This happened sometime later, in the yard at the Mill House, when he got me in the back of the neck after a dispute. Mum promptly smashed his gun with a hatchet, and I don't think even the makers could have put it back together. On returning home one day in the summer with Mum and her brother Tom, in the pony and trap, Uncle Tom found a grass snake by the front door. He dealt with it with his boot and, on looking back, it seems a pity that Clifford hadn't still got his gun.

Another of our exploits involved finding a wasps' nest on the corner leading up to Shapwick Hill, and Clifford, myself and others thought we could stop the wasps getting in or out by plastering the hole with wet mud. All went well until I realised I had got one or more wasps inside my shirt. I set off on the 100 yards or so for home, yelling with pain as I was being stung without pause, or so it seemed. Mrs Susan Williams (Banger's mother), attracted by my yelling, came out and advised me to get home as soon as possible. I really didn't need telling, and Mum soon got to work with the blue bag. I have had a healthy respect for wasps' nests ever since.

Mrs Tully of Home Farm, Shapwick, supplied Devonshire clotted cream, and Clifford and I occasionally had to pick up a jar after school for a treat at tea. We both liked cream and took turns in dipping a finger in the jar on the way home. We were chastised, and Mum said that what was left of the cream was not fit for pigs to eat. I can't remember being entrusted with that errand again.

One winter Clifford was seriously ill with congestion of the lungs and I well remember him yelling his head off when the doctor applied hot fomentations. His life was

SHAPWICK: The Mill House and the Mill (now a dwelling), 1982.

BAWDRIP: The Grange, where Granny March lived with Uncle Jack, 1977.

despaired of for a few days but fortunately he fully recovered. I recall having to stay in bed with the measles and not wanting to eat. However, my appetite returned and Mum boiled an egg with fingers of toast (soldiers) – I have rarely enjoyed a meal more.

Sometime after the Zeppelin raids on London had started I went to stay with Dad's brother, Uncle Bill, and his wife Lil, at 46 Russell Gardens, Lambeth. This was near Westminster Bridge and on the opposite side to Waterloo Station. It was in the top, or near top, flat in a six-storey block, reached by flights of steps as there was no lift. Before going to bed Aunt Lil insisted that cousins Albert and Myrah and myself were thoroughly washed in case we were injured in a raid and had to go to hospital. Fortunately there was no raid during the few days I was there. I had to get there by train on the Somerset & Dorset Railway from Shapwick to Templecombe, there changing over to the London & South Western which ran through Salisbury and Basingstoke and so on to Waterloo. Aunt Lil used to visit a street market known as 'The Cut' which was a sort of miniature Petticoat Lane. I remember seeing an Australian soldier, well and truly drunk, carrying on a heated argument with a woman in the street below the flat. He was addressing her in names I didn't understand and she was calling him a 'gentleman'. Looking back I think she must have been one of 'those'. I was eight or nine years old at the time.

Shapwick School

Clifford and I, now that we lived at the Mill House, only had about half the distance to walk to school compared to the Albion, and we came home for a midday meal. Mr Miles, a widower living in the schoolhouse adjoining, was the headmaster and Miss Peppard and Miss Bellringer the assistant teachers. Sometime before the end of the war in 1918, Mr Miles married Miss Peppard and they both continued teaching. Before this Miss Peppard was cycling daily from Westonzoyland, six miles each way, with Shapwick Hill and Pedwell Hill in between.

There were two classrooms, one for the infants with one teacher, and the bigger room for the rest where the other two teachers operated. I cannot remember the total number of pupils but I don't think it ever exceeded 60. Heating in both classrooms, when needed, was supplied by Tortoise slow combustion stoves which stood about three feet high and were surrounded by a metal guard. These were fuelled with wood, coke, etc. Some of the older boys used to be allowed the 'privilege' of sawing up the wood for the Tortoise stove during school hours. This was done at the rear with a crosscut saw. It suited the boys concerned fine, as they missed lessons but it was hardly what they went to school for. It was there that Mr

Miles once heard a commotion coming from the orchard behind the school where there were some hens. On investigation he found a dead hawk which a hen with chicks had obviously killed while it was attacking her brood.

The playground was of a fair size and of hard surface. When it froze in winter we had a very good slide diagonally across the whole area. Practically all the boys wore hobnail boots, which were ideal for the purpose. There was also a pond near Mr Wren's shop, and this provided sliding facilities out of school hours when the ice was thick enough. All the low lying ground on the peat moor became flooded in the winter months and when this froze it was possible to skate for a mile in a straight line between the Shapwick and Catcott roads. I could not skate but on a Wednesday afternoon, early closing day in Bridgwater, hundreds of people could be seen skating.

There was a party at Christmas for the kids of the village, held in the big classroom at the school, and I remember attending some of them. There would be a big, locally-grown Christmas tree decorated with the presents to be distributed. Sometimes there was variation in that the presents were put in a 'bran tub', i.e. a big container held the presents which were covered in bran, and each child in turn was allowed to feel for his present. I am not certain but I believe the funds for this were raised by donations from the villagers. A concert was occasionally organised, chiefly by Mr and Mrs Seamer,[6] and this took place in the school classroom. I took part in a couple of the plays and this involved a lot of rehearsing. Mr and Mrs Seamer did the coaching, and two or three nights per week were spent on this. Dad used to sing a song, one verse of which I remember:

> Poor old England, she isn't in the picture,
> Everything is foreign don't you see,
> The carpets on the stairs, the tables and the chairs,
> Are all made in Germany.
> Every night when I go in the parlour,
> Sleeping in a tiny cot,
> A little baby boy, his mother's pride and joy,
> And that's the only bit of English that we've got.

Blacksmith Beal used to sing 'Clementine', and Mr Wren from the shop used to do a sketch as a barber cutting a customer's hair. His son Ken was in the chair, and the dialogue between them provided the entertainment.

There was Sunday School with Mrs Seamer as the teacher. I attended this even after I started at Doctor Morgan's School. I was also in the boys' choir until I was about 14. There was choir practice every week but I wasn't the most regular attender, and I don't think the loss

6. The vicar and his wife.

SHAPWICK: The School, 1982.

of my vocal contribution made all that much difference when I left. I did not go on to join the adult section choir in which the voice of Miss Annie Tully predominated. She really could sing and I think would have held her own with some of the professionals if she had been trained. This section of the choir used to go round the houses on Christmas Eve, and I can remember hearing her voice above the rest at near midnight, after I had gone to bed, when we lived at the Bakery. The schoolboys did their carol singing round the houses during the daytime near the school. I went once or twice: we picked up a copper or two and some sweets here and there.

Another annual event for schoolchildren from about 1919 was a day trip to Burnham-on-Sea, the nearest seaside resort. This was about 12 miles, and the first time I went was by horse and wagon. Two or three of the local farmers each loaned a carthorse and ordinary hay wagon, plus the driver, and we set off by about 8am. Carthorses were never made to trot with wagons behind them, and it must have taken three or four hours or more to make the journey. I think we must have sat along the sides as I can't remember any seating. We couldn't have had long at Burnham, taking into account the travelling time and the fact that we were home before dark. Of course this was in the summer and probably on a Sunday as farmers were always busiest at this time of year with haymaking and harvesting. Other than necessary jobs, such as milking, farmers would not work on Sunday. One year, when the rain had spoiled so much hay, John Burrows decided to break the unwritten law on the first fine Sunday after a wet spell and gathered his hay. Within a week one of his carthorses died, and he never broke the rule again. He was quite convinced providence had meted out the punishment.

Later, the Burnham outing was by train from Shapwick Station direct to Burnham, via Edington Junction, Bason Bridge and Highbridge, where the Somerset & Dorset crossed the Great Western Railway. Mum accompanied Clifford and me on one occasion and, when we got to Burnham, she asked what I was chewing. It turned out to be the rind from the bacon which we had had for breakfast. On the return journey Mum was talking to the guard after we had taken our seats. He was slowly closing the door when I let out a yell as my fingers were being crushed. Had the door been closed with the usual bang I would have been minus the top half of about three fingers as the door was very heavy and tight fitting. Fortunately no damage was done.

FRED'S MEMOIR:

NEW HOME - NEW SCHOOL

Life at the Old Bakery 1918 – 1920/21

I think it must have been during the summer of 1918 that we moved from the Mill House to the Bakehouse at Shapwick which had just been vacated by the Pitcher family who had carried on the bakery business there. I suppose Father could have continued the baking as he was employed as a journeyman baker when he was a youth at Fenny Compton in Warwickshire. But he didn't and went on with his general buying and selling policy. Blackberries and apples, when in season, were two of his interests and he packed these off to London's Covent Garden market.[1] One of the firms he dealt with was Ridley & Houlding, and they would send baskets for the blackberries and barrels for the apples. The latter each held about a half-hundredweight of apples which were covered with straw at the open end at the top and kept in place by the small loops of rope attached to the barrel. When packed, the baskets and barrels were taken to the goods yard at Shapwick Station and loaded into the truck allocated. The supplies of blackberries came from the villagers who scoured the local hedgerows. The highest price I ever remember they got for their trouble was tuppence (2d) per pound, and much of the time only one penny. It took the most dedicated pickers all day to get 25lb. The apples came from the orchards of local farmers. The railway line, which ran from Burnham-on-Sea through Highbridge, Edington Junction and Shapwick on to Templecombe, was the Somerset & Dorset. It was known as the S&D, and the supporters of the Great Western Railway, much of which ran through Somerset, used to refer to it as the Slow & Dirty. The supporters, of whom I was one, knew it as the Swift & Delightful. In any case they always got our blackberries and apples to London and, later on, me to school each day at Bridgwater, more of which to follow.

Father bought a two-and-a-quarter horsepower Amanco Handy Man petrol engine and a saw bench, which were installed in the big shed at the bottom of the yard. The firewood was cut up in this way and, as elms were constantly being felled locally, there was no shortage of wood as the branches and tops were sold to the villagers for 1s 6d a time for each tree. This was no doubt a perk for the tree fellers. The trunks were collected by Turners, timber merchants of Meare, using horse-drawn carriages. To load the trunks onto the carriage, ramps were laid on one side and the horses stood on the other and pulled the timber up by means of long ropes. It was a very skilful job and it required well-trained horses that would stop at the right moment when the trunk was on the carriage, otherwise it would have been pulled straight over the top and down the other side.

SHAPWICK: The Old Bakery, 1980.

1. Cliff said that the blackberries were sent on to Manchester to be used in dye making.

As the scholarship scheme for entrance to Dr Morgan's School at Bridgwater apparently did not apply at Shapwick, it was decided I should attend as a fee-paying pupil. Dad took me to the school in the summer of 1918, and I remember being interviewed by the headmaster, Rev W.E. Catlow. Presumably I passed his oral test and was accepted to start in the second form on 10th September.[2] Grandmother March lived with Uncle Jack, Aunt Margery and their two children, Clifford and Marie, at the Grange, Bawdrip, the same house that brother Clifford opened fire on. This was just three miles from Bridgwater, and it was arranged that I should stay there from Monday to Friday while at school, riding my second-hand Coventry Eagle bicycle each way. Within a fortnight I got very homesick and, instead of stopping at Bawdrip after school, I kept going and arrived home within the hour, a distance of nine miles. There was only one way from now on and that was by the S&D from Shapwick Station, which meant a cycle ride of about two-and-a-quarter miles each way. The train left at 7.55am so I had to be out of the house soon after 7.30am. The first stop was Edington Junction where I had to change to the Bridgwater branch line. From the station at Bridgwater it was a mile or more on foot to the school at Northgate near Starkey Knight's brewery. At the start I was the only one from Shapwick Station but more boys joined the train at Edington and Cossington, and some girls who attended St Margaret's School in Bridgwater. Those I remember are as follows:

At Edington – Edgar Moxey and his sister Mabel from Burtle

At Cossington – Len Porter, Ivor Coombs and Vera Tratt from Chilton Polden
Stanley Mayne from Woolavington
Reg Sampson, Margery and Dulcie Stradling from Cossington.

The railway line, after leaving Cossington, passed through Bawdrip over the embankment which was at the bottom of Grandmother March's garden, and it became the habit to wave to her as she stood in the yard.

When the weather was too bad to cycle, the journey to the station was made by pony and trap and Mr Savage, his daughter Pat and Amy Davys joined the train, Mr Savage on his way to work and the girls to St Margaret's School. Alternate use was made of our pony and trap and the Davys'. In the winter months it could be very cold, and I often wondered how Cecil Davys managed to hold the reins without gloves. School started at 9am, and there was always enough time to get there if the trains were

2. Shapwick School's register records that my father left on 26th July 1918 when he was not quite ten years old. The cause of his leaving was said to be 'attending secondary school'.

'Our two boys' (left) in 1918, looking rather smarter than 'our two old boys' in 1985 at the Old Bakery. (Cliff returned there to live after giving up Bowerings Farm.)

punctual, which they almost always were. The train home left Bridgwater at 4.55pm, arriving at Shapwick about 5.30pm which meant getting home just before 6pm. There was always homework so there wasn't much spare time from Monday to Friday. The school fees were £1 8s 0d per term up to the age of 12, then £2 2s 0d. The railway season ticket was about the same. The railway line was single track except at the stations, where it was double track with a platform on either side. There was a stationmaster at each station, and at Shapwick it was Mr Ham who lived nearby. He wore uniform with gold braid on the peak of his cap. He was a highly respected citizen and was known as 'sir' to the staff of which there were two or three porters and one signalman. The latter was Mr Brown who also lived nearby. There were level-crossing gates, and these were operated by the signalman turning a big wheel in the signal box which was set high above the track and reached by a flight of stairs. When the train was coming there was a dinging of bells from the signal box, followed by the closing of the gates to road traffic and the signal arm being dropped. Mr Brown would then climb down from his box with a hoop-shaped affair with a leather pocket attached which contained the tablet authorising the train to go on to the next station. He stood close to the edge of the platform and held the loop aloft, with his right arm, for the engine driver to take. His left arm was stuck out to receive the similar hoop from the driver as he came past, still going at a fair speed before coming to a halt at the far end of the platform. I always thought what a dangerous procedure this was, especially in icy weather with slippery platforms, but I never heard of an accident.

The S&D coaches had opposing seats which ran the full

BAWDRIP: The railway bridge from where Fred used to wave to Granny March on his way to school, 1988.

BRIDGWATER: The Cornhill, 1975.

width as there was no corridor. I think it was possible to seat five aside, ten in all and, as we almost always piled into one coach, it was generally full for the last leg of the journey from Cossington to Bridgwater. The guard's van at the rear had a small protruding window of about six inches width on either side, and from this the guard could, while seated, look forward along either side of the train. One of the guards was a Mr Turner and, if we looked out of our window while in motion, he was almost always at his little window looking towards us. I don't think we ever got up to any pranks to incur his wrath but I think he regarded us as his biggest worry.

We weren't entirely innocent though and did get up to some mischief. There was a chocolate machine on Bridgwater Station which handled Reeves bars of chocolate. After putting two pennies in you had to pull out the slot which contained the chocolate. It used to be said that if you didn't pull the slot out to its full extent, but still enough to tug the chocolate out, you could push it back in and get another out without payment. I expect I tried it but cannot recall it ever working.

After getting off the train in the morning there wasn't much time to spare during the walk to school but on the way home we could indulge in window gazing. On one occasion I was looking in Vinten's window in Fore Street with some other boys when I felt a whack across the ear. This had been delivered by a very sprawl-footed policeman whom we knew as 'Sammy Sad'. To this day I still don't know where I went wrong but we were all advised to be on our way. Of course we went, as it was not the custom at that time to argue with policemen. It wasn't everybody in Bridgwater who took to Dr Morgan's schoolboys, and 'Sammy Sad' was probably one of the dislikers. The reason for looking in Vinten's window was that they sold very good catapult elastic. Catapults were looked upon as forbidden weapons if in the hands of boys but nevertheless we had them. I always left mine at home but there were those in the playground at breaktime who did not. Each boy had a notebook in which the masters entered items to be charged to the parents at the end of each term such as textbooks, school caps and whatever else was required during the term. One morning the Headmaster announced he had received an account from the electricity works next door to cover the cost of replacing broken skylights. No proof was offered that DMS boys had caused the damage though it had undoubtedly been assumed that we had, as we each had a small sum entered in our notebooks to meet the bill.

During the dinnertime break at school we sometimes wandered down to the docks to try our hand at making flat stones hop across the water. We were apprehended one day and, after we had explained what we were doing, the man replied that if he caught us again we should be the ones doing the hopping. I can't remember trying it again as I'm sure he meant what he said.

There was no provision for meals at school so, in the early days, I took sandwiches as did most of the others who came from outside Bridgwater, and this was probably half the total of about 130. Later on a restaurant, which I believe was run by a Mr Phillips in Fore Street near the Cornhill, offered schoolboy dinners, as they became known, for one shilling, and I went there with many others. Of course I had breakfast and tea at home and by the time I got to it at around 6pm, tea was most welcome.

Pitman's pastry shop in Eastover used to sell a confection made with flour and jam known as 'manchets' and these were delicious. I have never met them since nor, for that matter the name, until it appeared on the TV programme 'Call My Bluff' in about 1978, and I knew the answer. Other shops I remember in Bridgwater were: Ballinger's cycle shop, Whaddon's ironmongers, Vowles the grocers in Eastover, Baskers the chemist and Markhams the tobacconist in Fore Street. There was a fruit shop in Monmouth Street, where we bought oranges, and a private house near the school where we bought homemade sweets. Round the corner was a shop run by a Mr Boobyer where we got more sweets and fruit, and at the end near Starkey Knights brewery there was a shop which I believe dealt in cycles. In Fore Street was the Midland Bank, and it must have been when I was staying at Bawdrip in September 1918, and before the end of the war, that I was given a letter to post for Uncle Fred. This contained something to do with his call up into the armed forces. When asked if I had posted it I replied that I had and in answer to where, I gave the location which turned out to be the Midland Bank's letter box. Uncle Fred was never called up so I suppose the letter got to Taunton eventually. In Wembdon Road was Acklands the newsagent, and during the lunchtime break I sometimes bought the Wizard, Sexton Blake, Nelson Lee and other schoolboy publications including Westerns, chiefly about Red Indians, cowboys and ranches.

When Bridgwater carnival came along in November of each year, all the shop fronts near the Cornhill were covered with tarpaulins and hosed down with water, and Admiral Blake's statue was completely encased in wood. This work used to go on for a few days before the big night and must have cost a good deal of money. It was reputed to be the best carnival in the country, and attracted people from as far away as Bristol. I can remember seeing the charabancs parked in the roads alongside the River Parrett. There was the procession of decorated floats through the streets, and the squibbing display proper was held in the High Street. The squibs were attached to long poles, and these were held aloft by men standing in the middle of the street. There were dozens of them, and somehow they always managed to get them all going at the same time.[3] There were also fireworks being let off along the route of the procession, and this often led to injuries by burning among the very closely packed spectators lining the pavements. I went a few times up to the time I left home in 1930 but it wasn't a spectacle that I really felt like making a round journey of 18 miles to see. We preferred our own bonfire at Shapwick in one of John Burrows' fields at Manor Farm. He used to make a pile in the middle of the field of all the year's hedge clippings, and when the night came the bonfire was a good 12 to 14 feet tall. The village kids whose parents could afford it brought their own fireworks, and a most enjoyable evening followed. During the time the bonfire was being prepared wild rabbits made it their home and, within a few minutes of lighting up, they quickly emerged and ran off into the night. They were always too fast to be caught.

We had a school football (soccer) team consisting mainly of fifth and sixth formers. Among our opponents were Huish School, Taunton, Sexey's School, Blackford and the Blue School, Wells. I never got into the team and I only ever saw one or two matches which were played in a field near the Wembdon Road. We played football in the playground during the winter months and cricket during the summer. The wicket was marked with chalk on the brick wall.

The most important event to occur while we were still at the Bakery was the end of the war on 11th November 1918. We were all lined up in the playground (about 135 boys), and at 11am the flag was run up whilst we stood in silence. Dr Catlow said his piece and, after singing the national anthem, we returned to the classrooms. The chief effect of this was that the two lady teachers, of the total of seven, were soon replaced by masters who had been called up during the war. Mr Ambrose was the first form master, Mr Hazard in mine, the second, Mr Gillard the third, Mr Cuzenor the fourth, Mr Storey the fifth, and Mr Templeman the sixth. They all had specialist subjects and interchanged in the six forms as required. I can't remember exactly how it worked but Mr Hazard took woodwork, Mr Gillard maths, Mr Cuzenor languages, Mr Storey history and geography and Mr Templeman chemistry and physics. The subjects taught were arithmetic, algebra, geometry, English grammar, French, Latin, history, geography, chemistry, physics and

3. 'Squibbing', a tradition commemorating the Gunpowder Plot of 1605, is a practice peculiar to Bridgwater Carnival and still takes place – though with certain Health & Safety amendments.

Dr Morgan's School, March 1920: FCJ is tenth from right, front row.

woodwork. There were no exemptions, and we all had to take every subject. There was one exception at morning assembly, and this was granted to a boy named Grimshaw who was a catholic. He was excused attendance.

After the Great War, British army diamond-shaped tanks were distributed to the towns to act as war memorials. It was probably during 1919 that Bridgwater's turn came. With pupils of other schools we were marched to St John's Street and lined up either side of the road. The tank arrived at the GWR station and, from there, it was driven under its own power to the chosen spot where it was to be sited in St John's Street. It came trundling down the street at a slow walking speed and stopped. The officer in charge, a Canadian, got out and addressed the crowd, saying what great pleasure it gave him to be delivering the tank to BridgWODDER. We also had our own war trophy in the playground at school in the form of a gun on two wheels. It had a short-rifled barrel of about six inches diameter, in which we used to deposit sweet papers. I think the gun must have been a trench mortar.

An incident which sticks in my mind occurred before we left the Old Bakery. One fine day, probably in the summer, an aeroplane flew low straight over the main road, past the church and towards the station. I saw it turn just about at the bottom of the village and come back up even lower. It was obviously going to land, which it did in the field known as the Quarry Ground which was bounded by the road up Shapwick Hill and along the main road (A 39) at the top. From where I stood in the road outside our house I could not see the actual landing for the

trees, but I was among the first of the many to arrive at the scene. There was a gully running right across this field parallel with the A 39, and not more than 200 yards from it, and the plane came down safely in this short place which ran uphill. It was rumoured that the pilot had lost his way and was forced to land owing to lack of fuel. He stayed the night with Mr Brake at Hill Farm, the tenant of this field. Next day a motor lorry laden with two-gallon cans of petrol arrived, and I saw this poured into the plane's tank. The pilot got into the cockpit, then two men joined hands while one of them got hold of the propeller and they both pulled on it until the engine started. The point of the second man was obviously to pull the one holding the propeller clear when the engine fired. The plane was as near as possible to the gully and facing uphill. When the engine was opened it moved forward and, much to the relief of all those watching, not to mention the pilot, it took off just before reaching the hedgerow, flying up and over the telegraph wires with few feet to spare. It was said to have come from Yate, near Bristol, and that the pilot was now going to follow the lorry. It seems an unlikely story but the fact is I watched it for quite a long time before it disappeared from view over towards Glastonbury after having made some turns. I wrote to the Bridgwater Mercury in about 1975 but they had no record of it. It was a single-engined bi-plane but I recollect no markings.

Another incident I remember well happened while I was still at Dr Morgan's School. On 28th May 1920 or 1921, Clifford and I were birdsnesting when I fell from a tree while after a pigeon's nest. I well and truly fractured my

22

left arm near the wrist and, although dazed, I can still remember that the fractured bones had overlapped. Clifford walked me home saying that he was sure I should have to have my arm off. Dr Forden, who lived at the top of Shapwick Hill near the Albion, was sent for and he took my hand and arm in each of his hands and applied the extension necessary to put the bones back into line. He then put on two wooden splints, one either side, and bandaged the lot together, which was how it remained for six weeks. There was plenty of pain for the first two nights but then it went, and the feeling and grip gradually returned. I was away from school for a time but I think I resumed before the removal of the splints. At this time Clifford had started at Dr Morgan's and he brought home a note signed by all the boys and girls we met on the train to the effect that I was foolish to fall out of a tree. I agreed but that didn't stop me climbing to the tops of elm trees when the rooks were nesting in the years following.

SHAPWICK: **Top** - *Bowerings Farm, photographed by Albert Jennings on 20ᵗʰ May 1931.*
Bottom - *55 years later, looking very much the same.*

FRED'S MEMOIR:

BOWERINGS FARM

There was an empty farmhouse next door to Hill Farm, and Father became interested when he found that about 130 acres would be attached to it. It was part of the Strangways' estate [1] and hadn't been occupied since before 1900, so it was said. The last occupant was named Bowerings, and it became known as Bowerings Farm. I have since heard that, when occupied by the Bowerings, it was called Higher Farm. The farmhouse was in a run-down state, and most kids in the village, myself included, used to get in and play, as doors and windows were either broken or non-existent. There must have been considerable renovation before it was fit for us to move in, and I think this must have been during late 1919 or early 1920.

There were many outbuildings, including cow stalls, stables, a big barn, a cider house and some large sheds without doors for implements and hay to be kept in. The 130 acres included about 30 acres of arable land and seven or eight orchards amounting to about 13 acres all told. The rest was grassland, much of it near Loxley Woods, and overrun with rabbits.

Dad bought three carthorses from local sales, the dearest being £120.[2] The implements acquired included a single-furrow plough, a mowing machine, a hay wagon, a horse-rake and harrows. A carter was employed and a start made on ploughing the arable fields. The ground was very heavy so three horses were required on the plough, and one acre per day was the maximum achieved. With the best performance and fine weather everyday this would have taken a month, but it wasn't fine everyday and ploughing, which started usually in September, was seldom completed before November, and then was the time to sow the winter grain.

I cannot recall the first carter but the second was certainly Reuben Allington, who came from Dad's birthplace at Fenny Compton. Like many more, he had found himself tramping the roads at the end of the war. One morning, he crawled out of the straw in one of our outhouses, but how he found Dad after so many years I was never told. He occupied a bedroom at the farm and soon turned out to be the best ploughman in the village. He kept the horses in top condition but at very great cost in crushed oats. This

of course was only during the winter months as they were turned out to grass at other times.

The Handy Man petrol engine and saw bench were set up in the rickyard, where Dad and Reuben cut up firewood. On arriving home from school one day, I found Reuben had been taken to Bridgwater Hospital with a badly cut hand which he did on the saw when a log twisted unexpectedly. The injury proved to be so severe that his hand had to be amputated. He had arrived in Shapwick with only one eye, having lost the other in the war. I believe Dad got about £70 in insurance, which Reuben claimed was his, and off he went after being discharged from hospital. Later, a letter arrived from him to say that he had fallen on his feet in the Stroud district, but that was the last heard of him. That was probably in 1922 or 1923.

In about 1921 the bottom fell out of the apple business, and Dad was left with a lot on his hands. The apples were lying on the floor in a three-pole tent erected in the orchard at the rear of Bowerings Farm. I well remember how the tent eventually fell down on the apples, and the lot was lost. I never knew the exact sum but it must have been worth several hundred pounds and, from then on until I left home in 1930, farming was an uphill struggle, with debts mounting all the time. The financial loss of 1921 was never made good.

But for the financial strain I would probably have stayed at Dr Morgan's School until I was 16, but in the event I left at the end of the summer term when I was 14.[3] My first job was to hack thistles in one of the orchards near Manor Farm. George Williams was now the carter, and Maurice Durston looked after the cows, of which there were never more than six, the pigs, calves and other young stock. They both took part in other jobs such as haymaking, harvesting and hoeing the root crops in the fields. They were paid the going rate, which was £1 12s 0d, out of which each paid back 5d as their contribution towards the national insurance stamp of 10d per week. I am not sure if their cottages were tied to the farm, which meant rent free, or whether they paid this separately. Such rents were 2s 6d to 3s 6d per week.

Mum looked after the chickens, and occasionally Dad

1. Shapwick was unusual in that it boasted two manor houses, which belonged to different families, the Strangways and the Warrys.
2. This seems very expensive but it may well be correct because of the shortage of horses as a result of the First World War.
3. This was in 1922 and, as Cliff was too young to leave school, he returned to Shapwick School until 16th April 1924, when he was almost 14.

Hebditch egg-incubator and 'foster mother'.   Somerset Rural Life Museum

worked on the land. He couldn't take a full part in the rough going of the ploughed fields because of his disability, but he did his fair share in the hay and harvest fields. He was not bad at driving the pony and cart, buying a few eggs here and there and going to market. After leaving school I took over the running of our Hebditch sixty-egg incubator. I went with Dad and Mr Saunders, who took over the Albion from us, to Martock to buy the incubator. We went in Mr Saunders's trap, pulled by his mare 'Doll' which he would back against any in the district for speed. She certainly could move. Mum had not had much success with the incubator, and Dad couldn't get interested. It was heated by a paraffin lamp fixed to the exterior on the right side, and nearby was a water container from which a wick ran into the interior to provide the correct humidity. Access was through a glass-fronted door, which ran the full width, enabling the egg tray to be taken in and out. This held the 60 eggs which were marked with an X on one side and an O on the other. They had to be turned each day during the hatching period, and this is where the marking came in. The temperature had to be kept at 103 degrees Fahrenheit which was the most difficult problem despite the fact there

was a regulator that lifted a disc from off the top of the flue to let the heat escape when overheating took place. An ordinary flashlamp battery (flat type) was fixed to the outside and, by operating the switch, the interior could be lit by a small bulb as still used in torches. This was necessary to read the thermometer. The hatching period for hen eggs was 21 days, and a chart was provided by the makers showing the cooling and turning times. It was either once or twice per day that the tray had to be withdrawn and the cooling time advanced by one minute daily right up to hatching time, the turning being done at the same time. This was best carried out by wetting the tip of one finger. After about a week the eggs were tested for fertility which was done by holding them up one at a time against a special lamp. If they were clear, they were infertile and thrown out. It follows that it was advisable to ensure the right eggs were used in the first place. On the twenty-first day the door was not opened and, if all went well, cracks would appear in the eggshells, shortly followed by the emergence of the chicks. There was a gap of about two inches between the front edge of the tray and the glass door, and when the chicks hatched they made their way towards the light. They dropped over the top into another tray below, from where they were extracted and placed into a 'foster mother'. This was circular with a paraffin lamp in the centre and had a canopy of felt or some other warm material. The chicks would huddle close to the lamp except at feeding time when they came out from under the canopy. Mum did the feeding which consisted, of all things, of hard-boiled eggs plus breadcrumbs. When they were big enough to go without artificial warmth they were transferred to an ordinary chicken house. This method of hatching only took place in the spring and early summer, like the natural way of hens sitting on a nest of up to 12 eggs. I was reasonably successful and usually got about 90 per cent of live chicks from the eggs left after the infertile ones had been taken out. The hatching period for ducks was 28 days but we didn't breed many of them by incubator. This was left to the ducks themselves, of which we had some Aylesburys and some Indian Runners. Mrs John Burrows of Manor Farm had an incubator and she found she didn't have much luck so I used to take an occasional look and adjust the regulator and trim the lamp.

It was while we were living at Bowerings Farm, on 1st December 1922, that there occurred the biggest surprise I had experienced to that date. Brother Jim was born, at home, and I honestly had no idea that he was on the way.

As Mum would have needed some assistance, Dorothy French, a girl from Moorlinch, was employed as a general help and lived in, so I think she must have started some time before Jim was born.

The Farming Year

Throughout the year we had to work hard but never more so than during the ploughing season, which I remember clearly for its endless drudgery as I then saw it. In 1922 we had the three carthorses, two mares named Smart and Lively, and one horse named Sharper. After the fields were cleared of the harvest, we used a single right-hand furrow Ruston and Hornsby plough drawn by all three horses, two at the rear and the third immediately in front of the right-hand one. Both of the horses on the right had to walk with all four feet in the furrow which was quite an unnatural thing to do as the furrow was never more than ten inches wide. It is a wonder that they didn't trip up. Each field was ploughed in strips of 20 to 30 yards wide and, on making a start, sticks with paper on the top were placed at roughly 20 yard intervals, about half a strip in and parallel to one of the hedges, reaching the whole length. I am speaking of a four-sided field, mostly oblong as they were, with the start being made parallel to one of the shortest sides. The two rear horses had reins which the

SHAPWICK: Miss Strangways' clock and dovecote, 1982.

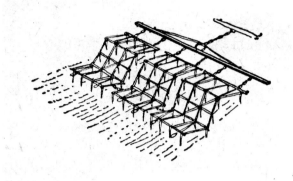

Harrow.

ploughman held, but the front one had to be led while cutting the first furrow and at each end thereafter. And this is where I came in as the ploughboy, as the leader of the front horse was known. I had to keep as straight a line as possible by watching the paper on the sticks and holding on to 15 hundredweight or so of straining, heaving horseflesh. The carter's reputation rested on how straight his furrows were and if the first wasn't straight it was impossible to correct afterwards. Mine were not too bad but by no means the best in the village. When the end, i.e. the hedgerow, was reached the front horse was led to the right and the two rear ones were guided by the ploughman right up to the hedgerow before they turned right. This was done so that as little as possible was left at the ends. These two ends were known as 'headlands' and were ploughed by going at right angles when the rest of the field had been done. Having turned right at the end it was turn right again so as to come down on the other side of the first furrow. This up-and-down went on until the strip was done and then another line of papered sticks was placed to mark the next strip and so on until the lot was done. The Shapwick land was very heavy, hence the use of three horses, whereas at Westonzoyland on the opposite side of the Polden Hills, two horses could do the job and no ploughboy was required. We were supposed to leave the stable by 8.30am and unhitch at 3pm during which time we should have ploughed one acre, but we never did. We had one twelve-acre field and we never got inside 15 days even with good weather, which was essential, as the plough soon got clogged up in the rain and put a stop to the work for the day. The only meal taken during a ploughing day was about 10.30 to 11am, consisting of bread and cheese and cider, while sitting on the beam of the plough. Each horse had a nosebag of chaff and a sack slung over its back, as they sweated quite a lot even though the weather was getting colder as autumn progressed. Occasionally when it was extra cold we made a fire of dried wood and toasted the bread and cheese on the end of a stick.

George Williams had served in the trenches in the Great War having said that he was 18 when he was only 16, but luckily he came through unscathed. On the 11th November 1922 we were ploughing at Catcott Edge, a good mile from home, with not a watch between us. We could only tell the time by listening for the clock which struck the hours at Miss Strangways'. At 11am we stopped in silence for our guess of two minutes.

After ploughing came the harrows which were drawn by two horses to break down the furrows. Then came the sowing of the seed which was done by a horse-drawn Massey Harris drill, hired or borrowed. This was not as long a job as ploughing as the drill was six to eight feet wide. The grain was thrown in the full-width box at the top, and the seed was sown in lines or drills by the ten or so tynes. The drill could be regulated to the amount of seed required per acre. With wheat this was one sack - about two-and-a-quarter hundredweight per acre.

Wheat, oats, barley and horse beans were sown in this way but for clover and grass, like crops, the seed was broadcast, i.e. to cover the whole area and not in drills as with grain. The implement used was known as a 'banjo' and it consisted of a small seed box and a disc affair into which the seed slowly trickled. Attached to the disc was a piece of wood, rather like that used in the bow of a bow and arrow, which was about a yard long. A piece of cord was attached to one end and then wound once or twice around the disc, the loose end then being attached to the other end of the bow. By operating the bow, left then

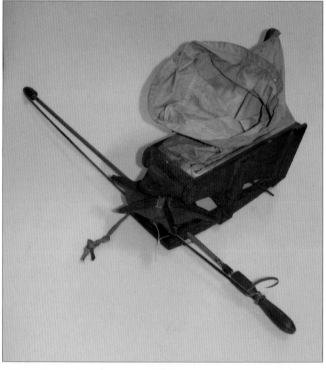

'Banjo', also known a seed fiddle.
Somerset Rural Life Museum

right, to its full extent the disc revolved and the seed was scattered right and left accordingly. The complete unit was strapped to the operator's back and he then set off parallel to one of the sides of the field, pulling or pushing the bow to accord with each stride he took. I think each starting point on the walk across the field must have been marked with a stick as it wasn't possible to see where the seed had fallen. Overlapping didn't matter but gaps would have occurred where no seed fell. In all cases after the seed was sown the area was traversed using light harrows and two horses. This was to ensure coverage of the seed, and all such work was usually completed before the end of November. Then the rooks moved in for their share of the spoils. Some farmers erected scarecrows, others employed boys to scare them off, but I never heard of a crop failure because the rooks had taken the lot.

During the winter the horses were kept in stables, and the first job for the carter at about 7am was to feed them and do the mucking out. When he got back to the stable at about 3.30pm after a day's ploughing, the feed had to be prepared, and this was done by cutting chaff from hay or oat straw (never wheat). The chaff cutter was driven by the petrol engine, which had now become a 3hp model Amanco as greater power was needed. A Turner oat-crushing machine had been installed which was also power driven. The mangolds and swedes were sliced in a hand-operated pulper and ours was a Bentall. All this took place in the big barn, where the feed of chaff, mangolds or swedes and crushed oats was mixed by shovel on the barn floor. The feed was conveyed to the stables in big, round, sloping-sided baskets that we knew as 'willy' baskets, which might have been a corruption of willow of which they were made.

After sowing time, attention was turned to clearing the yards of the accumulated manure, which was carted to one corner of whichever field it was to be used on and there piled in one big heap. The conveyance was a two-wheeled tipping cart, known as a 'putt', drawn by one horse. There it would be left to rot down for a year or more. In the spring holes would be scooped out and about a bucketful of earth, along with one marrow or pumpkin seed, was deposited in each. I can remember the heap in the twelve-acre field nearest home being covered with marrow plants. In the process of rotting down, these heaps got quite hot and, at lambing time, about January onwards, I have known Mum to bury a newly-born, half-dead lamb up to its neck. When it started to bleat loudly she knew the cure had worked and the lamb was restored to its mother. In very severe weather ewes about to lamb were brought into shelter but it sometimes happened that an unexpected hard frost upset the programme and the lambs were born out in the field.

Ewes generally had one or two lambs each but occasionally there were triplets which was one more than

Seed drill.

the ewe could feed. If a ewe had just lost her one and only lamb she became a likely foster mother. But it wasn't done by just putting one of the triplets along side her as she would bunt it aside. Then came the gruesome procedure of skinning the dead lamb and tying the skin on to the unwanted triplet. It almost always worked, and it was obvious the ewe was swayed by the smell. In some cases, especially when the ewe had died, her surviving lambs that could not be dealt with by adoption had to be hand fed; this was done with cows' milk in baby bottles with special teats which you could buy. I have done this and well remember how they wagged their tails and bunted just as they did with their mother. The feeding bottle had to be held tight.

Some land was set aside for spring-sown crops such as mangolds, swedes, potatoes and other root crops and, when the weather conditions had not permitted in the autumn, any spare land was used for spring-sown wheat, barley, oats, etc. The yield was never as heavy nor the straw quite so long. The ploughing process went on through the winter months whenever it was dry enough. Hard frost of course put a stop to ploughing so with this, heavy rain and occasional snow, there were never more suitable days than required.

The method of sowing spring grain was the same as autumn sowing but for mangolds or swedes there was a slight difference in that the rows or drills were wider apart. I believe the same drill was used with every other tyne or so blocked off, or there may have been a separate drill. We never owned either or I am sure I could now explain the mechanics more fully, but I recall there was a central shaft inside the seedbox running the full width, with a metal disc to each tyne, and to each disc several small cups about the size of acorn cups. When the drill was moved the shaft turned, and the cups tipped over at the top of their travel, spilling the grain into the tyne which was pressed into the soil at the bottom. And thus the seed was sown.

SHAPWICK: Haymaking – Fred is on the right.

There were two ways of sowing potatoes and we always grew an acre or more. If there had been time to plough and harrow the land, an implement like a plough was used with two turnfurrows which were joined and pointed at the front and gradually widened out for the two or three feet of their length. It looked like the modern snow plough and I have heard the name 'bouting plough' (that is how it sounded)[4] but this may have been the Somerset name – I cannot remember. The method of starting in order to get a straight line was similar to that I have described for ploughing with a boy (me at that time) leading the one horse. The result was a channel about six inches deep with sloping sides into which the potatoes were planted by hand at the correct spacing, 15 to 20 inches. I think the covering process was done by hand. The rows were spaced 24 to 30 inches apart and, after the first row, it was easy to see just where the horse had to be led to obtain regularity.

The other method was by ploughing in directly and this also entailed positioning the seed potatoes by hand. They were pushed as far as possible under the overturned furrow so that the horses did not step on them next time round. Slow though they were, the horses went faster than any one person could plant the potatoes, so that as many helpers as possible would gather to get the potatoes set in order not to hold up the plough. The plough would then turn over about three furrows before the next lot of seed

was planted so as to get the correct spacing of the rows. I often wondered how the potatoes ever managed to break through considering the unbroken five or six inches of solid earth covering them, but they did. After sowing, the harrows were dragged over to break down the tops of the furrows. A plot in our twelve-acre field was always reserved for this, chiefly as it was the nearest to home and because it was customary to allow those villagers who were interested the option of as many rows as required. They paid 2s 6d per row, each one about 100 yards long. They had to find their own seed and join in with the planting. From then on it was all theirs until they dug the crop in the autumn.

We had a horse-hoe, an implement like a plough but with two cutting blades set at sloping angles, which was pulled by one horse between the rows when the potatoes appeared. These blades could be set as to width, and the idea was to get as close as possible to the potatoes to remove the weeds. This was one row at a time, and the horse had to be carefully led walking up the centre of the row. If the horse was led off course the man holding the handles had difficulty in avoiding cutting the potatoes off. There was much criticism among the rival carters as to the straightness or otherwise of the other man's rows. Sammy Ayres, who later took over as our carter, always had a reply, which he frequently needed after I had led the horse, and it was that if they didn't grow in crooked rows

4. It was called a 'bouching' plough.

30

they wouldn't grow in straight 'uns either. The potatoes were rounded or banked up with the same horse-drawn implement which had made the planting drills, the horse having to be led between the rows.

The condition of the horses, especially in winter, was always a topic for criticism and leg pulling. If a boy was seen riding on a horse with ribs showing it was the opportunity for a rival carter to suggest that the boy should get inside and ride, the suggestion being that the horse needed filling out. I never knew who but it was rumoured that this ceased after an encounter between a carter and a boy. This is how it is supposed to have gone:

Carter on foot to boy on horse: 'Thee's wanna git inside he and ride.'
Boy on horse: 'If his ass was as big as thy mouth I 'ould.'
Carter: 'Any more o' thy cheek and I'll clout thee yer'ole (earhole).'
Boy: 'S'got catch I fust.'

As winter passed and the spring came, all the sowing was completed and, as the grass started to grow, those fields which were to be set aside for the hay crop were chain harrowed. This was a two-horse job, and the man walking behind the harrows guided the horses with the long rope reins as used for ploughing. The harrows were six to eight feet wide so it was not such a long-drawn-out job as ploughing. In fact nothing was.

About this time the horses would be turned out to grass, as were the cows that would have been kept in the stalls all night during the winter. They would however have been out all day, being brought in about 4pm, then milked and turned out after milking again in the morning. In the summer they would be milked in the field and the milk would be conveyed in churns by pony and cart. I don't think we ever had enough milk to sell to the United Dairies but some went at the door to villagers, and Mum made cheese, Cheddar and Caerphilly, which was later taken to Highbridge cheese market. As a delicacy she sometimes made cream cheese which was drained by being put on straw mats. We had a cream separator, an Alpha Laval, which I turned by hand many times. The cream came out of one spout and the skimmed milk out of another. The volume of cream was very much less than the skimmed milk. This cream was used to make butter which Mum did by constantly stirring. It was for our own use only. The cheese was made by putting the milk in a container up to four feet in diameter to which was added 'rennet'. This produced the junket effect and, when it had all set, it was finely chopped up into curds, the whey being drained off at the bottom by tap and fed to the pigs. The curds were put into cylindrical-shaped metal containers (vats) which were lined with cheesecloth, with a circular block of wood that just fitted in on top of the curds. These were put under a press and screwed down, and any excess liquid came out through the holes in the bottom of the vat.

I recall three sizes of these, two for Cheddar and one for Caerphilly. The small Cheddar, known as a 'truckle', was seven or eight pounds and the other, very much bigger, produced a cheese of over 60lb. Mum mostly made truckles. The Caerphilly vat was wide and shallow, about a foot across and two or three inches deep. This was said to be the favourite with the miners of South Wales, and Highbridge market handled a lot of it and, of course, Cheddar. After coming out of the presses the cheeses were stacked on shelves and had to be turned every so often. Caerphilly matured very quickly whereas Cheddar took some months before reaching prime condition.

As spring wore on the mangolds and the swedes came up and had to be hoed by hand as the rows were too narrow for a horse to walk between them. This was a back-breaking job, and I used to follow behind George Williams in the adjoining row. They had to be thinned out as they grew, and this meant reaching down and pulling out the unwanted ones by hand. Thinning out only had to be done once whereas hoeing continued as fast as the weeds re-appeared. I had difficulty in keeping up with George, and it was clear to see after a week or so who had done which row by the growth of the weed: mine had the most. When sowing mangolds or swedes it was usual to put a packet of carrot or turnip seed in the drill, and it was quite interesting to note where these appeared. They were spared at thinning-out time for table use later.

In the springtime the moles were very busy making their runs and turning up large mounds of soil. There was a market for moleskins so we could not let the chance of supplementing our very meagre income pass by. It was possible to make traps which consisted of a wooden platform about six inches by four inches with two U-shaped loops on the underside, one at either end, just big enough to let the mole pass through to push out the peg in the middle, which sprang the trap. This consisted of thin rabbit wire placed on the inside of the loops, up through holes in the platform and attached to a hazelnut stick of about four feet long, which was stuck into the ground and bent over to provide the power to catch the mole around the neck. The big disadvantage was that of the time taken to set the trap, and the fact that the bent-over stick could be seen from a considerable distance so that it often occurred that the person who set the trap did not get the catch. The alternative was a metal trap which acted on the clothes peg principle and this was set in the mole run with just the top two inches or so showing. Bridgwater ironmongers stocked them for a few shillings each. After skinning the dead mole, a most distasteful job to me, the skin was stretched out and nailed on a board with four nails, one in each corner, to dry. I forget how we disposed of the rest. The price varied between 1s 0d and 1s 3d per skin. Factories at Street and Glastonbury tanned and dressed the skins which made very good items of warm clothing, such as men's waistcoats.

Mowing machine.

 If the weather was right the first of the mowing grass would be ready for cutting in early June. A rainy May was very suitable for fast growth. When it was thought the weather would be fine for at least four days the mowing machine would be brought out having been looked over for adjustments, oiling, sharpening of knives, etc. Ours was a Deering, made in the USA and, like all the others, drawn by two horses. These were harnessed to the one long shaft, one on either side as with two- or four-horse stagecoaches. The carter sat on the machine and drove the horses by plough reins. The bed or cutting platform that contained the knife (approximately four feet long) was on the right-hand side; this knife, which was made up of triangular-shaped blades riveted to a steel strip, was driven backwards and forwards by a connecting rod coupled to one of the mower's two wheels. The far end of the cutting platform held a swath board, which was set at such an angle that it cleared the cut grass away from the next row to be cut otherwise it would have got caught up next time round. On going into the field the horses were driven close to the surrounding hedge all the way around, and this meant they trampled on the grass. Mowing was always done going round and round the outside, right to the finish. After the machine was well clear of the hedgerows, the first swath of grass cut was raked away, so that at the end the machine could be driven around close to the hedgerow and in the opposite direction in order to cut that grass which the horses had passed over first time around. No fewer than two, and sometimes three, knives were carried, and as each knife was never used for more than one acre, it meant they had to be sharpened as they became blunted. Sharpening was done by flat file, the knife being clamped to the top of the field gate. Each knife had two cutting edges, and I did the sharpening as well as the raking required to keep the machine going without hindrance. The best time for mowing was before the dew had gone as it was much easier for the horses. We sometimes got up as early as 4am to get as much done as possible before the sun got too hot. We only had a cup of tea before starting and if we were in the fields near Loxley Woods, Mum would bring our breakfast in the pony and cart between 8 and 9am.

She always managed to keep the bacon etc hot and the tea, which was in Thermos flasks. It was very satisfying to see her coming as I was quite hungry by then. We possibly cut anything up to eight acres at a time and, if the weather held, the swaths would be ready for turning in a day or so, depending on the strength of the sun. This was done by a swath turner which turned two swaths at a time and was drawn by one horse with the carter seated as with the mower. There was also an implement known as a 'hay tedder' which threw the drying hay about haphazardly. If rain came this turning process had to go on until it was dry enough to make the rick.

 The next move was to drive a horse-rake across the lot. This was another one-horse implement, eight feet or so in width and consisting of two big wheels between which were several curved tynes that gathered the hay into rows to be picked up later. The carter sat on a centrally-mounted seat and there was a hand lever and a foot lever to the right. The horse was driven from end to end of the field and, as it went forward, the tynes would pick up the hay. When the tynes were full, the foot lever and the hand lever were operated simultaneously to lift them up, and the hay was deposited in a heap. The shafts were attached to the front of the rake by a long rod which had a ratchet and a hand-tightened wing nut. This was used to adjust the height of the tynes from ground level in order to get maximum pick up of the hay, depending on the height of the horse.

 I recall a most alarming incident when riding the horse-rake in a field by the A39. I was using the youngest horse we had then, Nobbler, and he had only just been broken in. Near the end of the field, I was applying the levers when, before I knew it, I was thrown forward, down behind Nobbler's back legs and right back against the tynes with the hay. I shouted 'Whoa!' and Nobbler stopped at once. I crawled out, unhurt but very shocked and shaken. If the horse had bolted, as many would have done with the shafts around their heels, I dread to think what my fate would have been as every one of the many tynes was sharply pointed. I always made certain that the ratchet was done up tight after that as this was the cause of the incident.

 After the hay was gathered up into rows, the horse-drawn wagon with ladders affixed at both ends would come along for the hay to be loaded by pitchfork on to it. The boy in the wagon (me on many occasions) would then distribute the hay until it was fully loaded. The rickyard attached to the farm was always reserved for the grain mows (mow was the equivalent of the term rick which was applied to hay) but if there was likely to be spare space a hayrick would be made. In these cases it was necessary to load the wagon properly and sometimes to tie it down with wagon lines (rope) for the journey to the yard. If however there was no room, the hayrick would be made in one corner of the field, and the wagon could be loaded less carefully. There were times when a 'sweep' could be used in the small fields to get the hay to the site of the rick. This was a one-horse affair and had long, wooden slats which were dragged close to the ground thus gathering the hay up. To load the wagons two 'pitchers' were used, i.e. one man each side armed with a pitchfork, a two-pronged implement with a long handle. The boy on the wagon had a short-handled, two-pronged fork. Every time the horse was to be moved forward one of the pitchers would shout to the boy, 'Hold fast!' as he could well be pitched off if caught unawares on his springy platform. There was a fatality in the 1920s at Westhay or Meare when a boy fell onto the prongs of one of the pitcher's forks. Pitching progressively got harder as the height of the load increased. This job was always done against the clock owing to the uncertainty of the weather, and at the start of loading the boy on the wagon was sometimes overwhelmed, but his complaints made little difference. When the load got to 12 feet or more and pitching became much harder work some of the boys were known to say, 'Now then you buggers, let's have it'. Unloading was done by the same forks (short-handled) and this too was much easier in the initial stages but became harder as the rick grew and long-handled forks were used.

  Before the rick was started a base was formed of brushwood, hedge clippings, etc to keep it off the damp ground. The ricks were either square or rectangular in shape and occasionally round. It was necessary to decide on the size, and this was a skilled job. Too small and there would be surplus hay, too large and there would be a low, flat rick with much more roof to thatch when the time came. Maurice Durston was very good at this; he was one of the best rick-makers and thatchers in Shapwick. When the rick was completed with its sloping roof, it would be thatched with reed, i.e. wheat straw which had been combed out so that only the straight, firm bits remained. Properly done, this would keep out most of the coming winter rain, and Maurice D always did it right. To put the finishing touch he used to undercut the bottom two or three feet of the rick with a hay knife so that when the rain dripped down the sides it fell away before reaching ground level. The aforementioned assumes reasonable weather but if it rained when the hay was almost dry, it had to be turned and spread about until dry. If it rained again there was more turning, and in the end the farmer ended up with hay of poor condition, later to turn fusty, which had cost two or three times as much to make as good hay. With the hay not quite dry and still showing green patches, there was a tendency to take a chance and pick it up if rain threatened. This meant the danger of overheating in the ricks to the extent that spontaneous combustion occurred. Warning signs would be given by the rick 'steaming', which could clearly be seen, and the heat could be felt by climbing to the top. A further test

Swath turning.

was by inserting a long iron rod with a corkscrew end into the centre of the rick and withdrawing it after an hour or so. The old hands could tell by the feel whether there was a danger of fire and, if there was, the hay knives were got out and a gap cut right through the centre of the rick a yard or so wide. This was a fairly warm job but it was often the only way of saving the hay. We had a big three-sided barn between the barn proper and the cowstalls and this was filled with hay with no thatching required. When winter came, this and whatever rick there was room for in the yard, was the first to be used for the indoor stock. Some of the hay in the ricks in the fields was fed to whatever outdoor stock there was in the vicinity. A fence had to be erected round such ricks to prevent the animals helping themselves. Sheep were difficult in this respect as they could get through small gaps so the fence had to be close and solid. Hay used this way was cut out in squares about three feet each way and as much as you could lift in depth. Only as much thatch as required was removed at any one time in order to preserve the remainder. Hay not used this way, which was most of it, had to be cut out and carted home; this emphasised the need to get as much in the yard as possible at harvest time to avoid the extra work. Most farmers had an excess of hay which would be sold to dealers. They sent along haycutters armed with knives and a press into which they put about half-a-hundredweight, pressed it down and then attached two string bonds. These were called bales and were transported by the buyer. I think such ricks were always sold as they stood, as there were no weighing facilities that I knew of, unless they were at the dealer's end.

  The next big job after haymaking was harvesting and this started in late July or early August, the first crop being

Horse-rake.

winter oats, followed by the wheat, barley and beans. These were cut by self-binder, mostly Massey Harris, McCormick or Albion. They were drawn by three horses in the same formation as ploughing but with the lead or trace horse in front of the nearside rear. The rear horses were harnessed to the machine by one single shaft or pole running between them as with a mower. The carter rode on the machine with reins to the rear horses and a boy rode (not led as with ploughing) the front horse with a corn sack for a saddle. As the crops were always planted right to the hedgerows a way had to be cleared before the binder could start, not like mowing where the grass was trampled on. This was done by scythe, and a gap of about six feet wide was cut. The corn so cut was bundled by hand, about a dozen lengths of the straw being used as a bond. These were placed against the hedge, and the binder moved in. The journey to the field was made on two small wheels which were removed before cutting could start. This allowed the one big, wide driving wheel to drop to the ground. It was centrally placed beneath the machine, and at the far end of the cutting bed there was a small wheel. Upon moving off, the chain attached to the driving wheel worked all the mechanism, which was very complicated. The cutting blade moved back and forth as with a mowing machine. There was a windmill affair,

Threshing machine.

which revolved and pushed the standing corn back onto the moving canvas platform behind the cutting bed to coincide with the cutting motion. The corn was then picked up between two canvas sheets and conveyed to a point above the driving wheel where it was pressed into sheaves, automatically tied with binder twine and ejected to fall on the ground on the offside. The size of the sheaf was determined by adjustment of the pressure applied by the moving tynes or press bars. The cut ends were 'butted' or made level by machine so that they would stand squarely on the ground. The cutting bed was on the left, and when the boy on the horse got to the end of the standing crop he drove the horse on sufficiently far to allow the machine to clear the end. Then he turned left to bring the horse close in for the next cut. Binding was done the same way as mowing, that is by going round and round to the end. The sheaves which fell on the corners had to be cleared before the next round to prevent them being trodden in. (Later machines had a delayed action delivery system and the sheaf could be held and dropped well clear.) As soon as the cutting had begun, the 'stooking' could start. This was done by gathering a sheaf in either hand, planting them on the ground a foot or so apart and letting them meet at the top. About eight sheaves formed a stook and the purpose was to let them dry. It was also a precaution if the rain came, as the water would be shed as far as possible from the ears of grain. There was always much green weed caught up in the bottom of each sheaf; it was essential that this was dead and dry before going into the mow otherwise spontaneous combustion could occur, as with green hay. If there was no rain for a few days the sheaves would be loaded on to the wagon by two pitchers with the boy doing the stacking by laying the butts outwards. When there were few thistles, the loader used his bare hands but otherwise he used a short-handled fork. I had my fair share of this job. For the journey to the rickyard the load was tied unless it was a very short journey, and the loader would often ride on the top. The size of the mow was predetermined just as it was when making a hayrick: a base of branches from trees etc was made, usually a bit deeper than for hay, as any sheaves which got wet would yield substandard grain.

The completed mow was thatched and not touched again until the threshing machine arrived. This was done by contractors and there were two in the district: Alfred Labdon of Ashcott and Tom Harding of Moorlinch. A set of 'threshing tackle', as it was known, consisted of a traction engine, the threshing machine and a straw baler. Alfred Labdon had a Ruston & Hornsby engine and Tom Harding a Clayton & Shuttleworth, later joined by a John Fowler engine. Threshing was done during the winter months and was dependent on fine, dry weather. The thresher, mounted on four wheels, would be positioned alongside the mow and the engine lined up so that the long belt which transmitted the power was correctly placed. The belt went round the big flywheel of the engine and the very much smaller pulley on the thresher. The engine driver was on the scene by or before 7am to light up the boiler to 'get up steam', and threshing usually began by 8am. Two men on the mow pitched the sheaves to the first of the two men on the thresher who cut the binder twine bond as he passed them to the second man to feed them into the 'drum'. This revolved at high speed and a distinct 'whiz' could be heard when the sheaves and drum made contact. At the engine end the grain was discharged into sacks after passing through a screen which separated the small from the large.

The sacks were hooked onto the small vents which could be shut off as required. There were two for the top grain and, when the first sack was filled, a switch was made to the second. The first was removed by sack truck or carried to the barn, later to be weighed at two-and-a-quarter hundredweight before collection by the buyer. When carried, the sack was placed on a platform which hoisted it, by turning a handle, to the height necessary for the carrier to get it on his back. I carried a few when I was about 20 but always thought it was far too much weight. At the other end of the thresher the straw was discharged into a baler where it was tied with two bonds. These bales were put under cover for use later as bedding or feeding and, in the case of wheat straw, for combing into 'reed' for thatching and cider making. The chaff and dust were discharged onto the ground from in the centre of the thresher and one or two boys employed to take it to cover either in sacks or 'willy' baskets. This was easily the dirtiest job of the lot, and a bath was always necessary at the end of each day.

Thatching the hayrick.

The thresher had to be moved to each mow as one was completed and this involved some tight manoeuvring. The steering on a big traction engine was not nearly as positive as that on a car. The coal for the engine was supplied by the farmer as part of the contract, and the water needed was brought to the engine in churns. We had a running stream but on some farms the water must have come from the pump attached to the well. Alfred Labdon drove his own engine, Tom Glover the Clayton & Shuttleworth and Tom Harding himself the Fowler. Each thresher attracted labourers who travelled with it as no farmer had sufficient regular labour. The base or 'staddle' became the home of rats as they could easily get in between the gaps in the branches etc. They had a bonus in having their food supply of grain immediately overhead. When the mow had been lowered to about three or four feet, wire netting was placed all around so that the rats could not escape. They began to move as the last sheaves were picked up, and it was then that a terrier or two would be put in. They were sometimes joined by men with sticks who occasionally got the dog instead of the rat. Even so some rats got away by climbing the wire and getting under the next mow, perhaps to be caught the next time.

Hayricks.

A good proportion of the trees in our various orchards were

VINTAGE YEAR FOR CIDER

COMPETITION PRIZE WINNERS

By P. W. D. IZZARD

THIS is a vintage year for cider, as the results of the yearly competitions at the National Fruit and Cider Institute, Long Ashton, Somerset, announced yesterday, help to show.

In these competitions growers of cider fruit in the counties which form the province of Bristol University—the cider and perry counties of the west—send to the institute quantities of apples for milling.

The results do more than merely reveal what sort of a year it has been for cider. They also help to determine which varieties of apple and blends of varieties make the best ciders, and which are most suitable for growing in particular districts.

80 SAMPLES

Eighty samples were judged. The following are the prize-winners in each class:

Kingston Black.—1, W. Hill, Kittisford, Somerset; 2, H. Knight, Huntley, Gloucestershire; 3, W. R. Thomas, Nunnington, Hereford.

Sharp Varieties.—1, A. H. Walters, Newton St. Cyres, Exeter; 2, T. Fawkes, Stonehouse, Gloucestershire.

Medium Sharp Varieties.—1, R. C. Brook, Newton St. Cyres, Exeter; 2, E. G. Bryant, Taunton; 3. W. Ludlow, Westbury-on-Trym, Gloucestershire; 4, J. Maunder, Kings Weston, Somerset.

Sweet Varieties.—1, R. C. Brook, Newton St. Cyres, Exeter; 2, Burghill Trial Orchard, Hereford; 3, A. Pope, Crediton, Devon; 4, Burghill Trial Orchard, Hereford.

Bittersweet Varieties.—1, 2, and 3, H. C. Jennings, Shapwick, Somerset; 4, S. H. Osborne, North Cadbury, Somerset.

At a time when cider was so important to the farming community, an example from a local newspaper of 1934.

cider apples and, as there was an outlet for cider in the local public houses, Dad bought a cider mill and press. The mill for grinding the apples had a hopper at the top into which the apples were placed. This had a shute at the bottom which could be withdrawn to allow the apples into the choppers immediately beneath. Some of these were two wooden cylinders with bits of metal, like nails, sticking out. They were placed close together across the mill and when turned meshed into each other like cog wheels. The apples were chopped up in passing through and then fell in between two big rollers which crushed them into a pulp, before falling into a big wooden container. This type of mill was made by two firms at Mark, near Highbridge, one Wensley and the other Day. They had a big flywheel on either side attached to which was a handle, and they were turned by two men who had certainly earned their money by the time they had pulped about 15 hundredweight of apples which was the norm for one 'cider cheese' as it was known. Ours was converted for use with an engine by Blacksmith Beal who took one of the flywheels off and fixed a pulley wheel. It did the job but as we were going to use it continually from about September to November and it wasn't really designed to be turned so fast, Dad bought a Denning, made at Chard, to be machine driven; this had all metal choppers and rollers. The top of the hopper on all these stood six feet or more from ground level, and the apples had to be tipped in from baskets as grinding proceeded, but there was always a stop or so before the cheese was completed, as the man making the cheese got overwhelmed.

The press consisted of a wooden bed about four feet square with sides four or five inches deep, at the front of which was an outlet or spout about six inches wide to allow the juice to run into the big wooden trough. Above the bed was either one single or twin screws and these were wound up to their maximum height at the start. After ensuring that everything was clean the pulp was transferred to the bed by a wooden shovel, there to be shaped into layers. This was done by using an L-shaped affair made of two pieces of wood, about two feet long by four or five inches deep, joined to form a 90-degree angle. It was placed about four inches in from the walls of the bed, one corner at a time until the first cake had been formed by packing the pulp as tightly and evenly as possible over the whole surface. This was then covered by 'reed' which is wheat straw combed out clean as for thatching, care being taken that it had been well harvested and was not musty. The cut end of the reed was laid so that it slightly extended over all four edges of the cake, then the juice would fall into the bed and not over the edge. Then followed another cake slightly inside the first and so on until about eight cakes had been built. The result was a heap with sloping sides and juice trickling from the ends of the reed and finding its way into the trough. This was left to settle until the following day when pressing could start, which was done by two men lifting a wooden structure weighing about half-a-hundredweight on to the top of the cheese. It was about three feet to three feet six inches square and about six inches deep, counting the cross bracing, and slightly overlapped the top of the cheese. This was called the 'volleyer' which I think must have been the Somerset corruption of 'follower'. By this time much juice would have drained into the trough but when the screw was applied it came gushing out. Care had to be taken to ensure it didn't run over the sides, because some pulp always got into the channel at the base of the cheese and had to be cleared. Ours was a single-screw press which was turned by an iron bar a good six feet long. When the pressure built up two men would be on the end of the bar and even then would operate in 'jerks'. Due to the restriction of space and the structure supporting the screw it was only possible to turn the screw about one quarter of a full turn before removing the bar and placing it behind the next notch. There were four notches on most screws, fixed at the bottom of the thread. The threaded part of the screw ran into a big baulk of timber fixed to the upright on either side of the press. Some presses had a very big metal 'boss' instead of four notches, with two holes through the centre which in effect gave four positions, into which a long, strong, wooden pole was pushed to provide the leverage for turning the screw. When the cheese had been reduced to about half its original size the 'volleyer' was removed and about three inches was cut off each side of the cheese with a hay knife. This was then put back on top of the cheese and the pressing process followed once more. By far the greatest amount of juice was squeezed out in the first pressing but most locals insisted that the best cider was that which came last. If there was no hurry to get on with the next cheese it would be sheared a second time, possibly yielding a gallon or so. To clear the bed the pomace, as the pressed-out fruit was known, was cut into four sections with a hay knife and stored for use as animal feed. The trough was subdivided with a strainer in the partition so that the section with the lid on top contained the juice ready to be put into the barrels. This was done by carrying it in wooden buckets to the cider house next door and tipping it into the 108/120-gallon barrels which stood upright on baulks of wood (jibbing). Dad bought the barrels from a wine importer in Bristol and they were mostly 'port pipes'. It was obviously cheaper to sell them in the UK than return them to Portugal for refilling. We had one or two known as 'rum puncheons' which held about the same but they were lower and squat in appearance.

The barrels were filled right to the bunghole in the top and the bung left out. After a few days natural effervescence or fermentation started to occur and this could be heard as the juice came bubbling out of the bunghole, bringing with it bits of pulp which had escaped the strainer in the trough. It was left on top of the barrel and, when fermentation finally ceased, the top would be cleared of all the accumulated scum and the bung put in the hole. Cider made from Morgan Sweet apples could be drunk as soon as fermentation had finished but was never

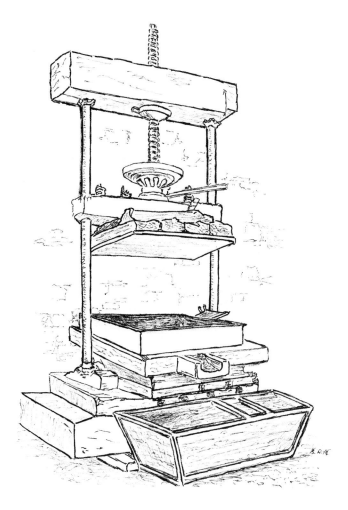

Brian Hutchings   *Cider press.*

regarded as top grade. That made from Hangdowns, Kingstone Blacks, Dabinetts, etc improved with keeping.

The Long Ashton Research Station, part of Bristol University, ran a competition for cider and, in order to take part, the entrant had to send one ton of apples, depending on the class, i.e. sweet, medium sweet, dry, etc. They paid £4 per ton which was well above normal price. The cider was made at the Institute in the autumn and, early in the spring, came tasting and prize-giving day. Dad entered two or three classes and was awarded prizes in about 1928. I drove him up to Long Ashton in the Citroen to enjoy a good day out and to receive the prize certificates. In the Institute orchards they carried out various experiments, and one I well remember was the effect Khaki Campbell ducks had on the apples. The ducks were fenced in one particular orchard and the fruit produced there was well ahead of that where the ducks were excluded. This was said to be due to the ducks eating up the grubs of the woolly aphids before they got into the trees via the trunks.

Once, while we were at Long Ashton, ICI put on a demonstration in a field which contained the stump of a fairly large elm tree. Gunpowder had been planted around the stump and when we had all been told where to stand, the plunger was pressed and up went the stump, roots and all, leaving a gaping hole. The amount of gunpowder was said to be 12 ounces and it was explained how many days it would have taken so many men to do the job with hand tools.

Dad went on to exhibit until about 1932 when I was in the police, stationed at Gloucester. PC Harold Stoneham who was stationed with me was a Bristolian and had been on a home visit to his parents where he had bought the Bristol Evening World. Next day he asked me, 'Is thy old man Henry Charles Jennings from Shapwick?' I said that he was and he then gave me the paper in which the headline was something like 'Mystery Apple Sweeps the Board at Long Ashton'. H.C. Jennings had been awarded first, second, third and highly commended in one class but nobody knew the name of the apple. I think it had a name attached later. Sometime before I left home in 1930, someone from Long Ashton brought a portable filtering plant to Bowerings Farm and ran one of our barrels through the wood pulp which was the filtration agent in the container. There was a glass tube so that the clarity of the liquid coming out could be judged against that still in the barrel. The difference was amazing, and Long Ashton said that if this could be done and the cider bottled, there would be a market for it. They bottled some and Dad kept a few for several years; eventually the cider came out like sparkling Champagne. Due to the financial strain this could not be followed up. Dad finished up not being able to sell it to the pubs even at 6d or 8d a gallon, as the brewers eventually got wise to the fact their pubs were selling less of their own beer than they were of someone else's cider, so they put the stopper on. After the 'mystery apple' affair Bulmers of Hereford visited the orchards and took cuttings or something similar from the trees. Pity they hadn't offered a partnership.

FRED'S MEMOIR:

SHAPWICK

Village and People

About this time Shapwick boasted a population of around 300. There were 14 or 15 farms, one general store (Mr Wren), a sub post office (the Misses Harvey), a butcher's shop (Mr Durston), a police station (PC Gould), a smithy (Mr Beal), a carpenter's shop (Mr Barnett), and one public house, the Griffin's Head [1] (Mr Chick). This was adjoining Shapwick Station [2] and not much used by the locals, as it was over two miles away. The nearest, the Albion, which we vacated, was in the parish of Ashcott, and those of the population who could afford the luxury of beer were customers there. The big houses were Shapwick House, the Manor House (also known as the Down House), the Lawn and the vicarage. [3]

The crossroads at Shapwick were formed by the churchyard wall on one corner and, going clockwise, the police station, then the house occupied by the Hooper family and on which the parish notice board was fixed, and on the last corner a house in which the Hucker family lived. This house, however, was pulled down in the early 1920s and the corner rounded off, due no doubt to the increase of road traffic.

The roads were made of stone and there eventually came a time when they needed resurfacing. At such a time loads of stone, both large and small and mostly quarried in the Mendip Hills, were deposited at the side of the roads where the grass verge was sufficiently wide to take it. Two such points were at the Firs, near the Albion, and the other near Whiteditch Cover between the Shapwick and Moorlinch turnings off the main Bridgwater to Glastonbury road. Later, along came the stonecracker(s) armed with hammers of varying sizes and a kind of hook on a handle to hold the stone in place when the hammering started. The stone was cracked into small bits about the size of hens' eggs. These were stacked in what eventually became an oblong-shaped, flat-topped pyramid. After sufficient had been cracked to about two or two-and-a-half feet high the stonecracker would place a sack on the top where he would sit. Then he pulled each stone towards him and broke it up, stacking it behind him as he went. When finished it was quite a work of art and perfectly shaped. They certainly took a pride in their work. The next job was to lay it on the road, and for this purpose a steamroller would arrive towing a four-wheeled wooden caravan and a water cart. The caravan was the residence of the roller crew, usually two men, for the working week which was Monday to Saturday. The

SHAPWICK:
The crossroads, 1977.

1. Demolished.
2. Closed in 1966.
3. Shapwick House belonged to the Warry family and is now an hotel, whilst the Manor House, owned by the Strangways, is a school for dyslexic children.

SHAPWICK: The Manor House, 1979.

rollers were owned by private contractors, and in the Shapwick area this was nearly always W.W. Buncombe of Highbridge. W.J. King of Bishops Lydeard, near Taunton, did most of the work in their area. I cannot remember that Somerset County Council owned any of their own. The job of laying the stone was done by the council workmen, and I think they did the whole width in one go so people driving along the road would have to travel over a rough patch for a few yards. Then the roller went back and forth until the stone was all packed down tightly, and it usually covered the whole width in two goes, one side at a time, until the whole length to be repaired was completed. I forget how the water cart was refilled, though it must have been frequent, as water was sprayed on the road, and the engine needed a fair amount to keep its boiler topped up. Tarmac hadn't arrived by the time I left home in 1930, and the verges and hedges were still covered in white dust.

About half of Shapwick was owned by Miss Strangways, who lived at the Manor House, while the remainder belonged to the Warry family. It was said that there was a feud between the two families to such an extent that they didn't speak to one another. Colonel and Mrs Warry occupied Shapwick House and the Misses Warry lived at the Lawn. The Manor House and Shapwick House employed a staff of servants, a chauffeur, a gamekeeper and gardeners. It was always assumed that Miss Strangways was by far the wealthier. Her house, although large by any standard, was smaller than Shapwick House and probably cost less to maintain. She lived alone except for the retinue of servants mentioned above. Occasionally she ventured out riding her horse side-saddle but I never knew her speak to a single child in the village. She certainly didn't to me. She was the rector [4] and as such had her own private pew in the church, not in the nave with the rest of us, but in the chancel between the choir stalls and the altar. She even entered through a private door at the east end so she didn't come within yards of ordinary worshippers at the west end. As her entrance door was near the main entrance gate she was out and halfway home before anyone else got near the gate. As the rector this was her privilege, or so I suppose. The Warry family worshipped in pews in the nave like the other villagers.

4. In the 1927 Kelly's Directory, Miss Strangways was referred to as the 'Rectorial Lady of the Manor and Rector'.
5. The date of the fire was 15th December 1920, according to the Bridgwater Mercury of 22nd December.

The vicar at this time was the Rev C. E. Seamer, and he and his family were living at the vicarage when, in the winter of around 1921, it caught fire.[5 opposite] I recall looking out of the bedroom window and seeing flames high in the air at about 7am. The fire brigade had to travel from Glastonbury, six miles distant. The fire engine was horse-drawn and, as this was a very frosty morning, the journey took twice as long as normal owing to the horses slipping. When they eventually arrived, the nearest water was well over a quarter-of-a-mile away in a pond. The inevitable result was that the house was completely gutted with most of the contents going up with it. Dad is said to have been the last down the stairs before the collapse. He was one of the many villagers who did their bit in getting out as much of the furniture as possible. The Rev Seamer, his wife and son John took the front half of one of the farmhouses, Manor Farm. No other farmhouse in the village could have offered suitable accommodation. A new and smaller vicarage was built on the old site, and the Seamers eventually moved back.

The other farms I remember were Hill Farm (Mr Brake), Pikes Farm, Northbrook Farm (Mr Tucker), Beerway Farm (Mr Jenkins), Kent Farm (Mr Davys), New Farm (another Mr Davys), Church Farm (Mr Marsh), Home Farm (Mr Tully) and Moorgate Farm (Mr Fear). There were two farms whose names escape me – they were both down on the moor and at least 200 yards from the road leading to the station. They were occupied by brothers of the Loader family. In winter when the floods came they were surrounded by water, and flat-bottomed boats came into their own. Four of the farms were occupied by people of Devonshire origin. John Burrows was the tenant at Manor Farm, and he spoke with a Devon accent. He married a Miss Vigar of Pedwell. There were three sons

who I refer to in the section/chapter on cricket at Manor Farm. It was a mixed farm of arable and grassland. James Davys was at New Farm and he too spoke with a Devon accent. There were two children, Herbert and Amy, both older than me. Herbert attended Dr Morgan's School at Bridgwater but he had left before I started there in September 1918. Mrs Davys gave me a school cap which he had barely used, and it was of much better quality than those issued during my time. Amy later married and went to live at Burnham. Herbert married a Miss Griffiths of Lockhill Hall, Ashcott, and used to travel from there to work on the farm on his Triumph solo motorcycle, which could be heard in the late afternoon slogging its way up Shapwick Hill. It was possible to count the exhaust beats. The marriage broke up and so too did the farming business. Herbert went to work for the AA in Wiltshire, and I don't think I ever saw him again. This was about 1928/29.

At Home Farm were Mr and Mrs Joseph Tully who both spoke with a pronounced Devon accent. There were four children, Annie, Bessie, Violet and Joe, in that order. They were all probably born there. Joe was a few years older than me, and I think he had already left Shapwick School when I started there in 1915. He was the only one to marry and he took over Hill Farm, next to Bowerings Farm, in the early 1930s. He specialised in sheep breeding. There were no children. At the time of writing (January 1978) Violet and Joe's widow are the sole survivors living in Shapwick. Annie's name was linked with that of Wesley Jenkins, a bachelor of Beerway Farm, but nothing came of it. Violet walked out with Bill Durston for a while but nothing came of that either. Home Farm was a mixed farm, on which the girls and Joe all worked, and work they did, milking, haymaking, etc. Joe

SHAPWICK: Shapwick House, 1982.

probably became the best thatcher of hayricks and grain mows in Shapwick. Also working there was Alan Duke who lived in. He had served in the 1914-18 war. He came from the Stoke St Gregory district, and it was there that he was buried when he died.

Kent Farm was occupied by bachelor brothers Jimmy and Cecil Davys, nephews of James Davys of New Farm. They did not speak with Devon accents and I think were born there. Their parents were from Devon but I can't remember them. James married a Miss O'Hare, a hospital sister who was Irish, soon after the end of the First World War and there were two or three children. Mrs Davys tragically died of cancer about 1930, and Jimmy soon after took his own life. Cecil used to ride a high-powered solo motorcycle, Harley Davidson I believe, and he was a bit of a tearaway. On one occasion in the early 1920s one of the British R series airships passed over Shapwick heading north. Cecil and pillion passenger gave chase and got as far as Cheddar before losing sight of it as it passed out of view over the Mendips. He emigrated to Australia in the early 1920s with Vic Saunders, one of the sons of the family who took over the Albion from us. Before I left home in 1930, it was reported that Victor had been drowned in a swimming accident in Australia and, as far as I know, Cecil never came back. Kent Farm was also mixed, and it had the only water wheel I remember in Shapwick. It was driven by water which collected in a pool fully two or three hundred yards away on the south side. It could only be used when the pool had been filled by the streams from Loxley Woods direction. I think summer use was very rare due to lack of water. In any case the advent of the stationary petrol engines during the First World War, such as Petter, Lister, Crossley and the American Amanco, provided a much more convenient power source. By the early 1920s I cannot recall a farm which didn't have one.

A very important service in the village was provided by the blacksmith's shop. It was run by Mr Beal (Bert), and he employed Bill Williams, George's younger brother, who was nicknamed 'Banger'. Each farm in Shapwick had at least three carthorses, plus one or two cobs or ponies, and these were all shod by Mr Beal. But this was only part of the business as he did running repairs to many farm implements, such as getting the mowing machines and self-binders in running order when the season came. He repaired the canvas on the binders, welded the broken cutting blades and rejoined fractured metal parts by drilling, plating and bolting. His skill was often used on the water wheel at Kent Farm as it neared the end of its days. 'Bonding' (fitting new iron tyres or bands to wooden wheels) was another job requiring his skill. For this the cold iron bond, previously made to fit over the fellows, or fellies, of the wheel was laid on a large horizontal metal platform, with pieces of Shapwick peat stacked closely around the inside and outside of the rim, and lit up. The bond eventually got red hot, then it was grasped with tongs held by Mr Beal and 'Banger' and placed on the rim of the wooden wheel lying flat. When it had burnt itself into a good fit, cold water was applied until it was cool, and then it was anchored by pins.

He made all his own shoes from the long strips of metal he kept stacked in the shed at the rear. The horse nails were in packets marked 'Mustad' and of Norwegian or Swedish make. When the roads became dangerous through ice he fitted 'frost' nails which protruded whereas ordinary nails did not.

He always kept a large grindstone and, on this, the scythes, reap hooks, axes, etc were sharpened. The person owning the implement, or his employee, was expected to turn the grindstone to which water was first applied. When new, these were over three feet in diameter, very heavy and quite hard work to turn, especially when 'Banger' was holding the edge to the stone, as he was very strong. There were two forges with bellows attached and a water trough at the foot of each, in which the hot shoes etc were cooled. It was said that immersion in this was a good cure for chilblains but I never tried it, although I always had chilblains in the winter. Mr Beal mixed his own brand of embrocation which he sold for applying to stiff joints, both human and animal. He never revealed the secret but turpentine was easily detected. Each weekday at about 11am he walked the 100 yards to our cider house where he partook of his bread and cheese and a cup of our cider. He was a very good friend of Dad's and I remember that when I called on him after Dad's funeral in January 1950 he openly wept. He was about Dad's age, and he went on for a few more years.

The contrast between the lives of the rich and the poor in Shapwick was stark but it was all taken for granted at the time. The male villagers worked mostly on the land as carters, ploughmen, cowmen and general labourers. They lived in hovels for the most part, and how they managed to bring up a family of kids (and they all had anything from four to eight or more) I shall never know. Poor old Alfie Ireland, who used to limp past the Manor House twice daily on his way to and from Tullys' farm, was a case in point. He was very crippled but had to keep on ploughing etc, which I know from experience to have been hard work. One of his boys, Clifford, about my age, used to attend school with me, wearing his father's left-off boots,

almost worn out, of course, and about three sizes too big for him. He was known as 'Trotters' for obvious reasons. I have often thought what a one-sided affair this was, and I am sure Miss Strangways could easily have given each farm labourer an extra ten shillings per week which would have meant the difference between bread and jam and meat or cheese. True the labourers lived in tied cottages rent-free and also had the chance of the occasional rabbit. Little wonder that some of them used to turn to poaching. Firewood was fairly plentiful which they took advantage of. They certainly could not afford coal.

Shapwick Heath (or Moor) is one of the few places in the British Isles in which peat is found. This was quite a thriving industry, and those engaged in it rented their bit of land from the Strangways or Warrys. In the summer they cut out the blocks which were, when dried, to be used as fuel. After drying, the oblong-shaped turves (approximately nine by six by two inches) would be stacked in ricks alongside the road, or on whatever other high ground was available, until required when the winter came. Then the two-wheeled horse-drawn high carts came on the scene and these were loaded with about 1,000 turves, which were hawked around the local villages and towns and sold as fuel. Much of it was loaded onto railway wagons at Shapwick Station for destinations far away. In the flooded winter the turves which had not been brought up to the road had to be loaded onto flat-bottomed boats and punted up to the pick-up point. As a result of the constant digging the level at either side of the road was several feet below road level, which was why there was so much flooding. However, there were times when even the road was flooded.

With the end of the war the men who had served

SHAPWICK: Blacksmith's Lane, looking towards Bowerings Farm, 1986.

SHAPWICK: Forsters, Jim Pole's house , 1979.

gradually returned to Shapwick. I think it a fact that no man who joined up from Shapwick was killed in action, and that was most remarkable considering the heavy losses. [6] From the adjoining village of Pedwell two out of the three Stevens brothers who joined up were killed, and there were probably others as well. Of those I remember who returned to Shapwick were the Barnett brothers, Victor and Percy, Sammy Ayres, George Williams, Jack Durston, Percy Argent, Walter Brewer, Reg Davis and Alan Duke. The Barnett brothers worked in their father's carpentry business, Jack Durston joined his brother William in the butchery business, Percy Argent worked in the bakery, and the rest worked on the land with various farmers. I believe Reg Davis joined the Lincolnshire or Leicestershire police but he didn't return to Shapwick.

As in all villages, Shapwick had its fair share of characters who stood out from the rest for a variety of reasons, good or bad. One was Dickie Gardener who was a bit older than me and the eldest of four boys. He lived with his parents, Harry and Lena, in one of the cottages in The Row. Harry was employed on one of the farms. When Dickie left school he went to work for John Burrows at Manor Farm, and he acquired a reputation for his own method of letting off twelve-bore shotgun cartridges. He would open a five-bar gate slightly so that the cartridge fitted between the gatepost and the gate. He then shut the gate so that the cartridge was held in position. He applied the point of a nail to the percussion cap and clouted the nail with a hammer, and the cartridges were fired just as they were in a gun. How he never got killed or seriously injured still remains a mystery. How he

obtained the cartridges was also a mystery as he certainly didn't buy them on his pay. I met him once with two or three Primax cartridges in his possession. These were superior to the Bonax we normally used so I persuaded Dickie to swap. When caught letting them off soon after and being questioned by Mr Burrows as to his supplier, he said Fred Jennings had given them to him. I satisfactorily explained my way out of that, and I think that was also the end of Dickie's exploits. His brothers were Edmund, Lewis and Amos but they never got up to any of Dickie's tricks.

 Jim Pole was a labourer and I believe was employed by the county council on roadwork. He lived with his wife and fairly large family at the thatched cottage in Bridewell Lane.[7]   The kids at school used to chant a ditty about him: 'Jim Pole shears hedge and throws the thorns upon the road. Motorbikes and motorcars come along and have punctures. Jim Pole pays expenses, if not goes to gaol.' I never knew him being summoned or going to prison on that account but go to prison he did in about 1921 when I was travelling to school by train. He was charged at Bridgwater Court with ill-treating his wife and was sentenced to imprisonment at Shepton Mallet Gaol. He travelled from Bridgwater to Shepton Mallet on the 5.10pm train which I came home on, and I remember a policeman standing at the carriage door to ensure that no other person but he and Jim Pole entered the carriage. When I left the train at Shapwick, Jim Pole was looking very sorry for himself as the train pulled out. By the time he came out of prison his wife and all the children except the eldest boy, also called Jim, had left and gone to live in

6. According to Cliff, no one from the village was killed in either of the two world wars, which is why there is no war memorial. Such villages have come to be known as 'thankful' or 'blessed'.
7. The cottage is called Forsters and remains the only thatched building in the village.

Sussex. Jim and son Jim stayed on in Shapwick just about long enough for them to get their passages booked to Canada, and that is the last I ever heard of them.

The only postman I remember at Shapwick until about 1924/5 was Johnnie Godwin (nicknamed 'Tit-Pont'), and he lived in the house adjoining the village hall. He wore uniform with the flat-topped helmet of the time and he walked. He had a very wide area which took in the outlying farms such as Northbrook, Manor and Kent, each up to a mile distant from the post office. He also covered the Griffin's Head pub at Shapwick Station and the two farms which lay off the main station road. He was a bit curt in manner and was not the most liked of Shapwick's citizens. The story used to be told of how Cecil Davys of Kent Farm was at Shapwick Station one day with a horse and cart when he offered Johnnie a lift, which met with the reply that he didn't want a lift in his so-and-so cart. Cecil repeated the offer later when it was raining heavily, and this time Johnnie said thanks very much, whereupon Cecil said not likely and you can bloody well walk. This was said to be quite true, and I never heard it doubted. Johnnie Godwin's brother and their father lived in Shapwick. The father, nicknamed 'Spitter', lived in one of the semi-detached stone cottages near the Mill House and he used to walk to the post office opposite the church once a week for his pension. It was said you could always tell when he had been by the tracks he left behind, hence the label 'Spitter'.

When the Misses Harvey ran the post office they had a horrible little terrier dog which sat inside the shop on top of the letterbox and snarled every time a letter was posted. One day, when I was about six years old and living at the Albion, I was going home from school, and he planted his teeth in my seat without any provocation. Miss Harvey apologised and scolded 'Fido', who was still going when I had left school. I often threatened what I would do to him if I ever caught him alone but the chance never came.

When George Williams left our employ about 1924/25 to take over Johnnie Godwin's job as village postman, Sammy Ayres became our carter. He lived near the Mill House with his wife and kids of whom I can name eight, from the eldest to the youngest: Bill (born around 1900), Rose, Hilda, Elsie, Sam, Nelly, Millie and Joe. Rose was the only married one at that time so where they all slept in their small cottage I can't imagine. Sammy was called up in the First World War and must have been over 30. He served in the trenches in France and was very badly wounded in the right thigh. He had a scar about as big as the palm of his hand, and I could see he had lost a fair amount of flesh. He walked with a slight limp but never complained. He smoked Klondike cigarettes, about 20 a day at ten for 4d. I imagine his disability pension bought his fags as his pay was the standard £1 12s 0d per week. He was very philosophical about life and rarely used bad language. He used to tell me to stick to the hard work of farming, otherwise I would be sorry in later years if the farm was allowed to go through lack of interest. I was never overcome with the thrill of drudgery (as farming was then) but I don't think that even superhuman efforts would have kept it going. Once, when Mrs Seamer, the vicar's wife, was making a goodwill call, one of the boys of the house abused and, I believe, struck her. The boy later broke his leg in an accident and Sammy's remark was that 'the Lord doesn't pay his debts with money'. He used to relate what a struggle it was in the 1900s after he married (at 18) to keep body and soul together with more kids coming along all the time. He worked for Mr Tully at the time and when ploughing on the Nidon he would leave the stable at about eight o'clock, not having had anything to eat since rising at about six. As he reached the end of the field farthest from home he would look towards

SHAPWICK: Sammy Ayres' and Steve Williams' houses after rebuilding, 1979.

45

the gate when turning round, to see if one of the kids had arrived with his breakfast. If they didn't turn up it meant that his wife hadn't been able to get credit at the butcher's and he had to wait until he got home in the afternoon for a meal of not much more than dry bread. If I remember correctly this state of affairs only existed from about Thursday, when the 32 shillings had run out, until payday on Saturday.

I was the ploughboy with him for two or three years so got to know him very well, and I still admire the way he got on with the job of life, despite much adversity. Once we were ploughing at Catcott Edge when we came across a rabbit hole in the middle of the field. This could mean a dinner if the rabbit was at home so I bravely put my hand in and pulled out what was left of a rabbit. In a matter of seconds out came a stoat which Sammy and I chased. We could outrun it as it was handicapped by the stubble but, although we managed to turn it a few times, it beat us both to the hedge. In the same field on another occasion I surprised a hen pheasant which rose from the hedge. It was about 20 feet in the air when the stone I threw caught it in the breast, so we had pheasant for dinner. In an adjoining field Sammy and I were ploughing when the plough share passed right over the top of a mole which at once started to dig into the side of the furrow. I think Sammy had the skin of that one which was worth between 1s 0d and 1s 3d. Sammy Ayres left us in 1927 when Uncle William came to the Mill House and he took over the ploughing etc. For a short time I was the ploughman with Clifford leading the front horse but I can't quite place the date. I never rode on the seat of the binder but I did much of the grass cutting, possibly after Uncle William arrived, and Maurice sharpened the knives.

Perhaps the most memorable character was Ralph Hancock who was not actually a native of Shapwick. In the early 1920s Colonel and Mrs Warry, who had no children, left Shapwick House to live in a place they had built on the edge of Loxley Woods and overlooking the parish of Greinton. (Shapwick House was taken over by a family I believe were named Griffiths and I think they, like the Howes at Ashcott, had been involved in the shipping business in South Wales.) Ralph Hancock came to be their gardener and he and his wife and two children lived in a cottage adjoining Shapwick House and known as the Island. He was recognised from the start as of very good education and was said to have also been involved in the shipping business in South Wales but not very successfully. I don't know if he gave up the gardening job entirely or whether he was part-time only, but it wasn't long before he became involved in catching rabbits, and Shapwick had plenty. I think Dad was responsible for selling the rabbits through various sources and that Mr Hancock got so much per head of the proceeds. The ferrets and other equipment for the job were kept at our place and, on several occasions, I went along to assist in

the catching process. At the end of the day it was the custom to string the dead rabbits on a sapling, the front end on Mr Hancock's shoulder and the back end on mine as he always led the way back home. This would be anything up to a mile and, with 20 to 30 rabbits, the pole was a bit heavy. Being some inches shorter than Mr Hancock it always seemed to me that the rabbits slid towards my end of the stick and I had the lion's share of the weight. If I complained he would advise me to grit my teeth and stand bolt upright as this would make things easier. He was probably right but I was always glad when we reached home. I never saw anyone handle ferrets in such a fearless way, his theory being that if you hesitated when making a grab for the neck you were far more likely to be bitten. He came unstuck one day though when Mr Miles the headmaster was with us. The ferret got him through the tip of a finger and would not let go. Mr Miles produced a pair of small scissors he always carried and he stuck the tips between the ferret's teeth and opened the handles. This did the trick but the incident didn't deter Mr Hancock from handling ferrets in the least.

This method of rabbiting was to select a burrow which it was fairly certain the rabbits were using, then to cover all the holes with nets. A loose ferret would then be put in and, if all went well, the occupants, if any, would come dashing out and into the nets. Sometimes it wasn't possible to put a net over holes in the middle of a hedgerow, and the escapees from these were dealt with by shotgun. Very often the ferret would find a rabbit at the end of its underground tunnel from which there was no escape. In these cases the ferret would proceed to make a meal of the rabbit and, if left, would have gone to sleep afterwards. It was sometimes possible to locate the spot beneath which this took place by the noise that could be heard. Then followed the job of digging down, sometimes as much as two feet, until ferret and dead rabbit were recovered. If there was no such sign, the procedure was to attach a collar and thin line to another ferret and put it into the hole. This second ferret would join in the feast and, by digging and following the line, all would be recovered. But it was a long job and wasted much time, especially as it was also expected by the farmer who rented the land that all the earth dug out would be put back into place and left tidy.

Mr Hancock had a much worn 12-bore double-barrelled shotgun with outside hammers. About the first time he used it, it fell into three pieces, the fore end, barrels and stock all parting. To counteract this he used to press upwards with the left arm and downwards with the right when taking aim. This reduced the worn gap between the barrels and the breech block but the brass flange at the end of the cartridge still tended to squeeze out when the explosion occurred. In the field at the rear of Bowerings Farm were three large walnut trees, and in the autumn the rooks would come for their share of the nuts. They would land at the top of the trees and, after picking off a nut, would fly away. It was not possible to get near enough to shoot them out in the open, and the only way was to stand under the tree and await their arrival. Mr Hancock did this but he found it was not always possible to get a clear shot because of the leaves, so after a rook had alighted he stepped backwards until clear of the tree. By then the rooks were alerted and took off. Mr Hancock then found himself leaning backwards before firing. This worked well until one day the action of the hammer going forward when the trigger was pulled caught in one of his nostrils, and he was covered in blood as a result of a severe gash.

On one of the occasions when he was rabbiting on his own he got caught carrying the gun without a licence and in time had a summons to appear at Bridgwater Magistrates Court. To get there he borrowed a bicycle from Rev Seamer, and at the end of the hearing (fine imposed) he adjourned to the White Hart Hotel, Eastover, Bridgwater. He evidently had one drink too many and took the wrong bicycle for the journey home. The rightful owner saw this and gave chase shouting 'Stop thief!' This resulted in Mr H being pulled from the bike and sustaining a sprained ankle which landed him in Bridgwater Hospital for treatment. He satisfactorily explained his mistake, and Mr Seamer got his bike back. Mr H was limping for quite a while.

He frankly admitted he knew little about gardening but, during his stay at Shapwick, he designed a garden frame which was later to change his life style. [8] It was divided into three separate, equal-sized compartments with a bottom a foot or so off the floor. Beneath this he fitted a metal water tank which was stepped down so that when the water was heated the first compartment was the hottest, the second not so hot and the third the coolest. The idea was to raise seedlings in the first compartment and transfer them to the other two as they grew, and then into the garden. The tank was all in one but the first held the most water, the second two thirds as much and the last only one third.

Ralph Hancock's heater tank.

It was probably during 1924 that Mr Hancock left Shapwick and that was thought to be the last we should hear of him but he was to reappear in the summer of 1925 as I shall relate later. One of the last jobs he did before leaving was to gather in the cider apple crop for Dad. This entailed shaking the apples off the trees, either by climbing up and rattling the branches or by using a long ash pole. When they were all down they had to be hand picked and put into sacks under the trees, later to be collected by horse-drawn cart. He was paid 6d per sack of about one hundredweight and he could manage 15 sacks a day. He could hold his own with most of the villagers at their own task. His wife made some of the best shortbread I have ever tasted.

8. Did his time in Shapwick, as the Warrys' gardener, inspire Ralph Hancock to embark upon a highly successful career as a garden designer? That would be very gratifying for the village if it was the case.

SHAPWICK: The Island, where Ralph Hancock lived, 1982.

SHAPWICK: St Mary's Church, north side, 1979.

FRED'S MEMOIR:

VILLAGE ENTERTAINMENT AND ACTIVITIES

The Shoot

As all the land and dwelling houses in Shapwick were owned by either the Warry or Strangways families, all the game (i.e. pheasants and partridges) belonged to the owner of the land. They decided who should be allowed to shoot, or otherwise catch and kill, these birds. Each land-owning family had a gamekeeper, and part of his job was to detect anyone breaking the rules, as neither the Warrys or Strangways ever allowed the locals to take any. The actual offence was poaching, taking game without a licence, which cost £3 per year in addition to the usual gun licence which cost 10s 0d per year. But it was no use buying a game licence if you hadn't got the landowner's permission. On Warrys' estate the pheasants were reared from eggs which were bought at pheasant farms. When the breeding time came round in the spring, farmers and others who had spare broody hens would loan or hire them to the estate to incubate the eggs and bring the chicks on until they didn't require a mother, when the hens would be returned to the owners. The chicks were hand fed by the keeper and it used to be said that they would feed from the keeper's hand right up to the time when the shooting season started on 1st October. They were bred in hundreds and were mostly Mongolian and very pretty in colour. There were some naturally wild ones, known as golden pheasants, but these were a very small minority. The shooting was let annually to a syndicate consisting of all the local gentry in the Bridgwater district, directors of Starkey Knight and Ford, the Bridgwater brewery, and various other notables. On the morning of a shoot they all gathered at Shapwick House, together with the keeper and some of the locals who acted as beaters. Their job was to walk through the woods and across the fields in order to drive the pheasants into the air and into the path of the army of shooters who advanced in line. This went on right up to the end of the season in February, and during the whole period several hundred brace of pheasants were killed. (They were always referred to as brace, never in singles.) When we first had a car in 1925 I was employed to take the spare shooting bags and lunch baskets to a pre-arranged spot by lunchtime. It seemed no shooter was able to carry all the cartridges he would require to last the day when setting off from Shapwick House. It was a sore point with the farmers that these outsiders were allowed to come in for the day, walk over every field on the estate whether cropped or not, shoot at will at any pheasant or partridge, whereas any tenant trying it on ended up in the police court. But they didn't have it all their own way, and the full extent of poaching will never be known as those involved obviously kept quiet. I can relate my own experience which didn't really reduce the pheasant population much as I was always too scared of being caught. In any case our farm was on the Strangways' estate, and they did not go in for the syndicate shooting method, and the keeper was not very worried. In fact he existed in name only. However, Warrys' pheasants used to fly over our land as the fields were very interwoven, and pheasants knew no boundaries.

Warrys' keeper was Joe Clark, a shortish man with a limp but very active nevertheless. He was not the most liked person in the village, especially by those who fell for taking a pot shot at a pheasant or partridge, but he must have been regarded as a very good servant by his employers. We used to describe him in very different terms as he missed no chance of reporting anyone he caught taking a partridge or pheasant, which landed them in Bridgwater police court. Both Farmer Davys and Farmer Jenkins were caught and paid the penalty by being fined. There was a family at Ashcott very well known for their poaching prowess, and they were probably Joe Clark's biggest problem. Around 1925 the latter was on the trail after hearing shots being fired in a coppice near the Nidons when he claimed he was fired at. This was during the night-time in the winter, and he could not identify the persons involved. The incident was regarded as serious enough for posters to be issued offering a reward of £25 for information leading to the conviction of the assailant(s). No one was ever charged, but the general opinion was that it involved the Ashcott family. In fact, some time after, one of them admitted to Dad that they were involved but they only fired over Joe's head to stop him following. Joe was not a native of Shapwick, and I believe he came from East Anglia. He always referred to partridges as 'PORTridges', and he told Wilf Durston and myself that he did not want us disturbing his PORTridges when he found us walking across one of the fields near Moorgate Farm at nesting time. (PORTridges make their nests on the ground in grassland.) He had three children, Violet, Dorothy and, I believe, Joe, who all attended Shapwick School in my time. When he left school the son followed in his father's footsteps by getting a job as under keeper on the Greville Smythe estate at Ashton Court. About 1928 Joe Clark left and the job was taken over by Bert ...... who was just about as carefree as Joe was keen.

SHAPWICK: St Mary's Church, south side, 1979.

When he knew that I was to catch or meet a train at Shapwick Station in the Citroen he arranged for a brace of dead pheasants to be left in Ice House Cover for me to collect.[1] His reward was all the cider he required.

Bell Ringing

There were six bells in Shapwick Church ranging from treble 5cwt to tenor 12cwt. They were regularly rung until Miss Strangways put a barbed wire fence from the east end of the church across to the boundary wall by the road. She said the correct way to reach the belfry steps on the north side was by the main gate and walking right round the west end and back eastwards. This was about three times as far as walking between the graves on the east side, and, as the ringers would not give in, up went the fence, and so the ringing stopped. Most people thought what a pity it was that the bells were silent so when I was about 16 some of the younger element approached the experienced ringers such as Bill Sweet, Victor and Percy Barnett, who were still keen, to see if they would train us in the art. I joined in with Wilf Durston and his brother, Dick, and Bill Richards, amongst others. In the initial

stages the clappers were tied so that no sound was made, and this continued until we were able to gain sufficient control to follow in sequence. There were a few scary moments when someone failed to catch the rope and it swung all over the place until one of the old hands could bring it under control. I once saw the ascending rope catch under Bill Richards' boots and jerk him back against the wall. We eventually formed a team that was capable of ringing a peal of call changes, that is the change in the order was made when the call to 'Change!' was given by the captain. The changes (540 of them) were listed on a board which all could see so that each knew which bell to follow when the call came. The real art of change ringing is that the sequence alters at the end of each round which means each bell makes one complete 360 degree turn before being changed to follow the next bell in the order as outlined on the board. This means that the ringers must have learnt the order of the rounds as there was not time to look at the board with the change being made at rope's end and at 'sally'. I never reached this state of perfection before I left home and never had the opportunity afterwards to follow it up. We occasionally visited neighbouring churches to have a go, and I have been to

1. Before refrigeration, many manor houses had their own means of cold storage, which could be stone built or a deep pit dug in the ground. Both were packed with ice taken from frozen lakes or ponds, hence the term 'ice house'. The one at Shapwick House seems to have been underground, a suitably discreet place to deposit the 'contraband' pheasants.

Greinton, Moorlinch, Ashcott and Bawdrip. An annual event was the ringers' supper, which consisted of a meal and drink at the village hall, but it fell by the wayside, and I only ever attended one. I don't know how it was financed but I think it must have been by village subscriptions.

Early Radio

Around 1920/21 wireless sets became available to the public, and the first we had was a crystal set. There was a bit of crystallite material in a cup and a small spring with a pointed tip mounted on a bit of metal about three inches long which was hinged on a bracket. With headphones on, the tuning-in process consisted of getting the pointed bit of wire onto the most sensitive part of the crystal. 2LO was the radio station call sign, the one and only if I remember correctly. There were two or three coils (fine wire wound round some insulating material), and the theory was to move these about on their mountings until you got the best reception. In one of the boys' papers there appeared the instructions on how to make a crystal. The parts could all be bought in Bridgwater. I bought the crystal and cat's whisker unit which was all in one, plus the fine wire for the coils. This was wound on to two cotton reels which were placed on a wooden meat skewer and the lot mounted on a piece of wood about eight inches by six inches. It all worked fine, and it didn't matter in the least whether the cotton reels were close up or pushed apart along the skewer. We had two pairs of earphones at the start, and Clifford and I used to listen in, especially to the football results. The aerial was a most important part of good listening, and the higher it was the better. We fixed ours, a length of wire with insulators at either end, from the top of the barn to the kitchen chimney of the house. We later graduated to a battery set which involved valves that glowed when switched on.

The Village Hall

In the early 1920s someone got the idea of making a village hall out of a big barn just below the church. It belonged to either the Strangways or Warrys, and I think they must have provided the funds. The walls, roof and floor were all renovated, and there was a portable stage at one end and a good-sized balcony at the other. Functions which took place at the school were transferred here, and a very popular place it became. There were dances with the music provided by someone playing a piano but most popular were the whist drives. I think some of them extended over four weeks which meant the total score counted for the prizes, first, second, third and booby – the lowest. There were also partner whist drives in which you kept the same partner for the whole 24 hands. I graduated to play with Dad who was very good at card games of all

kinds. These activities only took place during the dark nights, from October to about February. Travelling players arrived on the scene, and I recall they put on, amongst others: Carry on Sergeant, Ole Bill and the Better 'Ole, and Maria Martin and the Red Barn. There were three or four players, all ex-soldiers of the World War who, like many others, could find no regular work. One of them was said to be almost stone deaf. They also performed at Ashcott Memorial Hall and here too dances were held but they were more ambitious as the floor was bigger and a small orchestra engaged.

At Harvest Festival time, usually in September, the church was filled with various offerings such as bunches of flowers, fruit, vegetables, home-made jam, pickles and so on, and all this was passed on to the Bridgwater Hospital. But as many villages did the same thing the hospital was landed with much more than it could consume before decay set in. It was then decided to auction the lot in the village hall, and this is one more job Dad did. Besides assisting with the transport from church to hall using our pony and float with 'Tom' in the shafts, he was also the auctioneer, and once or twice I did the recording of the item, buyer and price. The paying-up came at the end and the proceeds sent to the hospital. So as to boost the funds, the better-off in the audience, after having the item knocked down to them, would put it up a second time, which meant double or treble the selling price going into the funds. I often assisted with putting up and taking down the stage and arranging the seating.

One of the big houses at Ashcott was occupied by the Moss-King family when we first moved to the Albion, but during the Great War it was partly or wholly used as a convalescent home for wounded soldiers, and they could be seen daily in the village, dressed in their light blue coats and trousers. They each had a badge in the left-hand coat lapel, indicating they had been discharged as medically unfit for further active service. At the end of the war the house was taken over by a family named Howe, and I believe they were connected with the shipping business in South Wales. At all events they must have been wealthy for they built the Ashcott War Memorial Hall in 1919, opposite their own house. This was used as a dance hall and, on Saturday evenings, as a cinema. The films were of course black-and-white and silent. There was a piano accompaniment and almost all the seats on the ground floor and in the balcony would be occupied. There was usually one full-length film and a serial, generally of twenty parts. The Three Musketeers was one I remember. In common with most of the youngsters from Ashcott and Shapwick, I was in the audience. Above the stage at the west end was a billiard room with a full-sized table but that wasn't for younger folk. However, it was well patronised by those eligible. As a dance hall it was easily the best in any of the surrounding villages and on the occasions when catering was required, Uncle Walter and Aunt Soph dealt with that.

Motor Vehicles

There were no motor vehicles in Shapwick, other than the Strangways' and Warrys', until the early 1920s, and some of the first I remember were Farmer Wesley Jenkins' Model 'T' Ford and Farmer Jim Davys' (Kent Farm) Ford, Model 'T', I think, but which was certainly followed by a Citroen 11.4hp.

Of the motorcyclists, Cecil Davys, Jim's brother, and Miss O'Hare, Mrs Davys' sister, who lived and worked at Kent Farm, had solos. Cecil had a Harley Davidson among others, and Miss O'Hare I believe had an AJS. Herbert Davys, the son of another Jim Davys, of New Farm, had a Triumph solo. The two Davys families were related but I don't know how. Percy Barnett had a Raleigh solo, and Mr Wren had a two-cylinder Raleigh with sidecar attached. This was later replaced by a Calthorpe or Clyno two-seater car with dickey seat. Mr Seamer had a two-seater but I forget the make. These cars were open top with hoods attached.

Uncle Walter at the Albion had a car almost from his first day there and he used to do hire work, probably the first in the district. One of the earliest was a French La Bure open four-seater tourer. This was a bad starter and also had the habit of conking out on a journey, and sometimes it had to be towed home. I was present on one occasion when Uncle Walter turned the starting handle until he was completely out of breath. On such occasions La Bure became known as La Bugger. Later on he had a saloon-type Renault of 1912 vintage with the radiator behind the bonnet. This was very big and heavy and had a klaxon horn which Uncle Walter made good use of when going through Shapwick. I went with him and Dad to Wincanton Races in about 1920 and, for the first time, I saw the early version of Bingo. The proprietor set up his pitch and then offered strips of wood a few inches long on which were marked three numbers, all different. After selling the lot (about 6d each) to the customers he drew numbers, one at a time, from a bag, and the first to have his three called won the money. The boards were then handed in and another round started, unless a race was in progress. It was here that I first saw a racing fatality. A horse fell at a fence and had to be destroyed. This turned out to be a mare called Rathnally who had run second in the 1912 Grand National. This was on the old racecourse and on much lower ground than the present course.

About this time Bill Langford started a carrier service from Ashcott or Walton to Bridgwater, through Shapwick, Catcott, Edington, Chilton Polden and Cossington. He used a German BENZ (not Mercedes as now), with chain-driven rear wheels. There was a top cover and the

1910 20 h.p. MODEL T FORD
Three-seater Sport Runabout with body style carried over from the Model S Ford of 1908

Commercial card.

52

SHAPWICK: The Oaks, Butcher Durston's old house, 1986.

passengers sat in the rear in seats facing each other, four or five aside. He operated on Monday, Wednesday and either Friday or Saturday or both. Not only did he carry passengers but he also did any shopping required, delivered parcels, made payments into the banks, etc. It was a very good service and the old Benz was very reliable. At other times he catered for parties to the pantomime at Bristol etc. Uncle Walter later took over the same route with Joe Dibble as the driver. He used a converted Crossley Army Tender at the start and, later again, an International which looked more like the modern bus and held more passengers. I think Bill Langford must have given up by then as there could not have been enough custom to support them both.

The Wilts United Dairies of Bason Bridge came onto the motor scene early when they commenced a milk-collection service. One of the early vehicles was an Albion open lorry which was also chain-driven to the rear wheels. There were three or four stopping places in the village where a low stage was erected and on this the farmers put their churns of milk. The first was by the oak tree near Butcher Durston's shop. Farmer Broome, next door at Hill Farm, produced two or three churns of milk daily which Jack Exon used to convey to the stage on a four-wheeled trolley. The collection was once per day.

Around 1924 young Bill Durston of the butcher's shop acquired a new Ariel solo and Percy Argent a BSA solo, soon to be followed by Bill Cox of the bakery with a Sunbeam solo. This was one of the most expensive of its time and regarded as the best of the British bikes. Bill Durston had the bad luck to hit a bridge coming home from Cheddar which put the bike off the road for a time. I don't think Bill was hurt.

Sport

Dad had played a lot of football as a boy at Fenny Compton and later in the Metropolitan Police. He played on the left wing and used to tell of playing for Street soon after coming to the Albion. I have a recollection that Street played in the preliminary rounds of the FA Cup, and that Dad played in one such match. I doubt whether he had a hand in the formation of the Ashcott and Shapwick football team soon after the end of the war in 1918. The field chosen was the Old Windmill field on the left side, and almost at the top, of Shapwick Hill. It wasn't ideal as there was a slight slope from side to side but there was a match almost every Saturday afternoon against neighbouring village teams. The team was for the adults, and Percy and Victor Barnett were two of the

Shapwick players. One of the most formidable of the opposing teams was Walton, and I think they nearly always beat our team. The boys of Shapwick also formed a team, and I was the centre forward with Clifford on the right wing. He was easily the fastest on our side and was later to come second in the Somerset Schools 100 yards championship. It wasn't often we played other than among ourselves but one of our opponents was Ashcott boys, and once I recall we ended up fighting. Dad was almost always the referee for both the adult and boys' teams but I don't think he could have been there when we fought or he would have stepped in. I know I ran home as fast as I could with some of the Ashcott boys in pursuit as they were bigger than I was, but I was the better runner.

A cricket team followed some years after, and the field was on the main road at Ashcott opposite the house occupied by Henry Davys. (More of this later.) The same field was also used for the annual Ashcott and Shapwick flower show-cum-sports meeting. A tent was erected for the flower and vegetable show in which there was much competition and cheating, insofar as one or two of the competitors I could name used to collect the best produce of neighbours who themselves were not interested in the show. The sports events were right up Dad's street, not as a competitor, but as the chief organiser, handicapper and starter. There were the usual races from 100 yards to one mile on the track, and the marathon which started at the Cornhill, Bridgwater, nine miles away. Of the marathons, I remember one which a man named Chinnock from Misterton, near Crewkerne, was the first to finish. The track races attracted entries from Bridgwater, Glastonbury and Street as well as the villages. Mum used to make ice cream with ice and freezing salt which had to be brought from Bridgwater. This was sold to boost the funds, and real ice cream it was. There were sweet stalls, and the Betty family from Bridgwater were always there with their gingerbread stall. There was also a feature which I have never yet got to the bottom of: for a penny or so you could buy what must have been a hot air balloon of sorts. There was a kind of paper bag and, at the bottom or open end, there was something which, when lit with a match, soared off into the night sky. The light could be seen for miles, or so it seemed, as it got higher and higher and finally disappeared from view, usually in the Glastonbury direction. On looking back I think the flame must have come from cotton wool soaked in methylated spirit but it lasted for so much longer than I would have expected. By the mid 1920s this event had died out.

I can remember that I won the high jump at about 4ft 8ins at the last meeting when I was about 16 or 17. Dad's championship jump in the Metropolitan Police was 5ft 2 and a half inches, and that was running straight at it. I used to approach from the side as the fashion had then become. In my last year at Dr Morgan's School I was leading in the high jump when I slipped on the wet ground

Milk transport.

and went under instead of over. I was hurt to the extent I had to withdraw, and there went the only chance I had of winning that event. In the track events at Dr Morgan's both Clifford and I were always severely handicapped having to give yards to boys who were our equals. I think Dad's fame must have got to the handicapper's ears, and the name Jennings meant scratch position always. I was in the first three once in the obstacle race where there was no handicap except the obstacles, like going through a ladder, under a sheet and picking an apple out of a bucket of water, using teeth only. This meant you had to push the floating apple to the bottom of the bucket so as to get a grip with your teeth.

Cricket was a very popular sport in Shapwick during the season and, when haymaking or harvesting did not demand working until sunset, some of the boys of the village met at Manor Farm, occupied by Mr John Burrows. In a sloping field adjoining the farm, a pitch was marked out with three stumps at the lower end and just one at the top end. This meant we batted one at a time, and the idea was to see who could score most runs. There were no sides as there weren't enough players. Eight to ten would be about the maximum and, besides Clifford and myself, there were Mr Burrows, his sons Raymond and Norman, and one or two of the Hazel boys and others whose names escape me. Mr Burrows was the only adult and probably the keenest of the lot of us. He did his fair share of bowling, and I am doubtful if his action would have got past a Test Match umpire. He brought his right arm up quite normally but when at its highest he slightly bent his elbow which gave the impression he was throwing. However, he wasn't very fast and I cannot remember any injury as a result. His son Raymond was probably the fastest and, with the slope in his favour, he certainly got up a bit of speed. There was never any question about being out by being bowled, but every other decision was open to argument, especially when the bowler claimed lbw (leg before wicket) which the batsman often denied. I believe the problem was solved by the opinion of the fielders which naturally always went against the batsman. It wasn't unknown for some disgruntled batsman to leave the field and go home. On one occasion one of the Hazel boys hit Clifford over the head with the bat but no damage was done.

I had been smoking cigarettes, mostly pinched from Dad's pocket, since I was about 12, and I remember being on the cricket field on the occasion of my 16th birthday and remarking that I could now smoke within the law. It wasn't until I joined the police that I found out it was not an offence to smoke under 16; it was just the supplier who was breaking the law.

Ashcott and Shapwick joined forces sometime in the 1920s and formed a cricket club, most of the players being adults of which Dad was one. I remember Dennis Farrow from Ashcott, a fine slow bowler, the Stevens brothers from Pedwell, Herbert and Rowland, and the Barnett brothers, Victor and Percy, from Shapwick. I first played for the team in about 1927, the year in which Uncle Bill left the police to live at the Mill House. His son Albert arrived with the reputation of being a fast bowler who had won two or three trophies as a boy in London. It was soon obvious that he was by far the fastest in the district and soon gained a reputation by snapping the one wicket in two and landing the bails farther away from the crease than had been seen before. Our playing field was at Ashcott adjoining the main road opposite Henry Davys' house, where the annual flower show and sports were held. It was like most village pitches, a bit rough and uneven despite being rolled. Albert exploited these conditions, and it was never certain where the ball would go after hitting the ground in front of the batsman. There was a fixture every Saturday during the season but we (Dad and I) couldn't always play as harvesting had to come first. Some of our opponents were Walton, Baltonsborough, Chilton Polden and Westonzoyland. I well remember playing at the latter when news came through that the American airman, Lindbergh, had crossed the Atlantic and landed in France, the first man to do so solo. Albert later got a job with either Clarks or Morlands and soon got into the first eleven. He was so successful that in about 1929 he was offered a trial with Somerset. I was there on the day when the teams were made up of the Somerset first and second elevens and one or two more like Albert, on trial. He must have been overawed by the occasion as he did not bowl nearly as well as he could. He was just as fast but was landing the ball about halfway down the pitch, and those which didn't pass over the batsman's head were hooked without mercy. When he batted he hit just one four and was then out. Needless to say he was not offered a contract. The vicar's son, John Seamer, was without doubt the best cricketer (batsman) ever produced at Shapwick. He became an Oxford Blue

and played many times for Somerset. He hit 77 (not out I believe) against Maurice Tate, the Sussex fast bowler, in his first game. John occasionally played with the boys' team, when home from school, and I remember he and I put on over 30 against Chilton Polden on their ground before I was bowled by Stan Chick. Ashcott and Shapwick first eleven were regarded as so good by the surrounding villages that they got together the best from each team and challenged us, which was accepted. It was an evening match played in a field by the back road from Ashcott to Shapwick. We batted first and, by the time the opposition got in, the light was fading. Albert soon got among the wickets, and when about five were down, all Albert's work, they said they would not go on unless Albert was taken off. Our captain declined, and so ended the match which we had undoubtedly won by default. I must add that any first-class umpire would have called halt in the bad light but we didn't indulge in such niceties, the rivalry being so intense.

BRIDGWATER FAIR

Bridgwater Fair was an annual event commencing on the last Wednesday in September and ending on the following Saturday. The amusements were all in St Matthew's field, off West Street. Some of the stallholders (those offering goods for sale) were in the field but many of them were on one side of West Street, and some of them spread their wares on tarpaulin sheets laid flat on the ground. Amongst these were people offering cycle accessories (bells, acetylene and oil lamps, brake blocks, chains, pedals, saddles, almost everything except the frame) and the harness for horses, plus the cleaning materials and the brushes and combs for grooming. The 'cheap jacks' who sold watches and the like did not have an open display but held them up one at a time and sold by the Dutch auction method, i.e. naming an inflated figure and gradually dropping down to the price described as a bargain not to be missed. They sold some but it was generally acknowledged that the best place to buy a watch was at a jeweller's. We used to get the odd bits for our bikes, halters etc for the horses and a lamb's foot pocketknife almost every year. These were 1s 0d each. The stallholders sold gingerbread, chocolate, sweets, kitchenware and china.

The amusements were the big attraction and once or twice while at DMS, I saw the big traction engines, the Burrells, Fowlers and the Garretts chugging along the Bristol Road, each with three big trailers and a water cart attached, the maximum allowed by law. The engines all had a big canopy over the top, supported on highly polished brass columns. They bore names like Earl Beatty and Lord Jellicoe and were mounted on solid rubber tyres, unlike the iron-shod wheels of the threshing engines and steamrollers. They were a sight which always appealed to me and they were remarkably quiet considering their enormous bulk. Some of them weighed up to 18 tons. Having arrived at the field a day or so before the Wednesday, the men travelling with each outfit set about the big job of unloading the trailers and erecting their particular piece. The roundabouts (carousels) varied, and I recall the switchback railway, the galloping horses and the chair o' planes. The big attraction for me was the organ which remained stationary in the centre. There were Gaviolas, De Caps, Chiappas, Hooghuys, Marenghis and Mortiers, and each front was adorned with the figures of men or women who beat time as the organ played. I remember one bore the plate 'Made in Liege, Belgium'. Some had a harsher note than others but, taken collectively, the modern equivalent of fairground music, with loudspeakers blaring much too loudly, isn't in the same street. In the case of the galloping horses the whole lot revolved around the organ but with the switchback only the cars moved round and round, up and down on the rails. The big names in the roundabout business who came to Bridgwater were Marshall Hill, Anderton and Rowland and Charles Heal. The traction engine stood within a few yards of the roundabout and was kept running to supply the electrical power needed for the scores of light bulbs and the organ. Each engine had a dynamo mounted on top of the boiler just in front of the cylinder(s), and the small pulley wheel was connected to the engine flywheel by belt. Cables connected the dynamo to the roundabout by being laid on the ground and they were very heavily insulated. A small stationary steam engine was sited near the organ and this drove the gallopers or switchback. The engine was started and stopped in accordance with the duration of the ride. The brasswork on the engines was kept highly polished all the time, and there was obviously competition among the drivers. Despite their weight they were rock steady when working stationary, and I once saw a driver balance a penny on edge on the hub of one of the big road wheels to demonstrate this.

There were many other attractions such as the helter-skelter, which was a tall tower with a shute running around the outside from top to bottom. After paying your money and being given a mat you climbed to the top on the inside. The mat was then placed in the shute, and you sat on it and away you went to the bottom, where the last few feet were horizontal so that you were just about stopped by the time your feet could touch the ground. There was always an attendant at this point to keep the landing clear for the next person coming down. I never saw it happen but there would have been a hot seat for anyone slipping off the mat.

The sideshows consisted of shooting galleries, hoop-la and coconut shies. I never knew its name but there was one stall which had five white-painted, tallish skittles placed together and they were very heavily laden with lead at the bottom. For tuppence you got three wooden balls and if you knocked three of the skittles over you got a packet of Players cigarettes worth 6d. With cricket balls it would have been easy for those with good aim but the wooden balls were so light that they bounced off the skittles, and it was only by catching them right at the very top that they could be knocked over. I must just have held my own at this. I don't think the shooting galleries offered prizes, the idea being just to find out how good you were. One target was a sort of ping-pong ball which floated on top of a spout of water with a slight rise and fall, making it difficult to hit. There were stationary targets such as clay pipes and glass bottles but it wasn't considered sporting to concentrate too heavily on these. When the ball was hit the attendant lifted it back into place with a long-handled spoon affair but when the pipes and bottles were smashed they were renewed by hand, shooting being stopped meanwhile. The rifles were .22 and fired real live ammunition.

There were various sideshows staged in tents where an entrance fee was charged. These included boxing booths and fortune tellers. Among the 'freaks of nature' I remember the 'Siamese twins'. On the canvas outside these were portrayed as two girls dancing but the reality inside was very different. It was a glass jar containing two babies joined together in some preserving liquid. I imagine they had been stillborn, and it was not a sight I wanted to see again. The boxing booth proprietors lined their fighters up outside the booth and invited members of the audience to participate, with the promise of £1 if they were still on their feet at the end of three rounds with their opponent. There were three or four to choose from, and the idea was to match the challenger with his weight or class equivalent. I never saw any challenger knocked out and I was convinced that they were 'plants' in the audience by the fact that when they stripped for action they always had boxing shorts on. The fortune tellers were always labelled 'Gypsy' something or other and sat outside the tent until a customer came along.

RALPH HANCOCK REAPPEARS

In the summer of 1925 Ralph Hancock reappeared without warning, driving a 7.5hp Citroen Cloverleaf three-seater car and accompanied by Eric Pittard, whom he introduced as his business colleague. He said he was on a business/holiday trip and could he camp in one of Dad's fields, which he did, and he chose the first one off Gazwell Lane near the Lime Kiln. During the two weeks he stayed, it transpired he had founded a business known as the Country Service Association with an office in Maddox Street, off Regent Street in London. It was on the lines of the Country Gentleman's Association (and really the poor man's version of it) which offered membership at a given fee and thereafter the privilege of buying by mail order almost everything on the retail market at a discount. I peeped in the tent one day when he was out and there were leaflets and catalogues of everything from wheelbarrows to traction engines. One evening I was making my way to play cricket at Manor Farm when I came upon the Citroen parked at the side of the road leading to Kent Farm. Ralph and Eric had gone off shooting nearby in Farmer Burrows' fields. I had known for a long time how a motor car worked, i.e. after starting the engine depress the clutch, engage low gear and let the clutch back. There was no ignition key in those days, just a push/pull switch for the magneto. Without further thought I started the engine and drove about 200 yards towards Kent Farm, turned round by reversing in the gateway by Alf Skinner's house and back up to where I had started from. There were three forward speeds but I don't think I could have gone through the gearbox as the distance was too short. However, from that day to this I have never had a driving lesson. Of course I had no driving licence but I told Ralph H what I had done, and he raised no objection as he had said he would teach me if he had time, so there was no offence other than the lack of a driving licence; compulsory insurance did not come until 1930. The Citroen Cloverleaf had a pointed tail, and the third seat was just like the dickey seat on most two-seaters but it took one person only who looked forward between the driver and the passenger. Hence the name Cloverleaf. Once or twice Dad was invited to the pub at Catcott so he sat with Ralph, and Eric was in the rear. I went as well

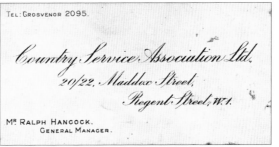

Ralph Hancock's London business card.

and I had to lie between the front wings and the bonnet and I think Clifford was on the other side. I don't recall that we went into the pub as we were under age, and Dad was fairly strict in such matters.

During his stay Ralph made it known that he would shortly be needing an office boy as he had a postal circular job in mind. I was asked to think it over and, as our kind of farming was still going downhill, Mum and Dad said they would not object if I chose to go. Uncle George, Aunt Rose and cousins Leslie and Ralph always spent their holidays at Bawdrip and when they came as usual in August, Aunt Rose said I could stay with them. They lived in Broughton Road, Stoke Newington, near where I was born, and Uncle George was still serving in the Metropolitan Police. So it was decided, and I went with them when they went back after their holiday. I don't think I was full of enthusiasm but I was prepared to try it. To get to the office in Maddox Street I travelled by bus, the Number 73 which went along Albion Road, Essex Road, past the Angel at Islington, down Pentonville Road, Euston Road, turned left into Tottenham Court Road, then right into Oxford Street. I got off at Oxford Circus, then walked down Regent Street and turned right into Maddox Street. This was very much of a change from ploughing the fields and scattering. The office was two or three floors up, and there were three rooms. Ralph Hancock had one, his wife, who was his secretary, had another and in the third, which was much the biggest, Eric Pittard, another adult male, two girl typists and I worked. The circular letter had just about started, and I spent a lot of time folding and placing in envelopes, sticking stamps, etc. I was told it would be to my advantage if I took up shorthand so I enrolled at a night school in Stoke Newington. My pay was £1 per week, increased to £1 5s 0d before I left, and I often wonder what arrangement Mum had with Aunt Rose as it was obvious I was not self-supporting after taking the cost of my keep and the daily fares, plus a bit of pocket money, into account. Not all my time was spent in the office, and I did all the errands. I remember being sent to a warehouse in the City to collect tea samples and to the spare parts depot of the Citroen Motor Company at

Hammersmith. Ralph H had a pushbike he didn't need and he said Dad could have it, so I was the one to take it from the office to Waterloo Station. I can well remember riding down Regent Street to Piccadilly, then to Trafalgar Square, Whitehall and over Westminster Bridge to Waterloo. There was a lot of traffic even then, and I had to be careful as the buses came a bit close when overtaking. There were several bus companies competing over the same route, not just the London Passenger Transport Board as now (1970s), and it was well known they raced each other to the most promising passenger stops. However, I survived, and there cannot be many people from Shapwick who have cycled over the same route. I had all meals with Aunt Rose except lunch, and Eric Pittard used to take me with him as he knew just which was cheapest and best, and this varied. One was Greek owned, another Italian and another where the meat portion was weighed on scales before going on the plate. To this was added pease pudding which was dug out of a saucepan with a wooden spoon and scraped onto the side of the plate. As time went on I got to addressing envelopes on a typewriter and turning the handle of the Gestetner duplicator, the stencils having been cut by the girls.

Cousin Leslie was 13 months my senior and he worked for a firm of estate agents. His brother Ralph was still at school. Leslie had a passion for classical music and had often attended the Sir Henry Woods concerts at the Queens Hall on a Sunday afternoon. It followed that I went with him to the first, and probably the only, concert there during my short stay. We met three or four of his friends there, who were about the same age as us. They were all Jewish and employed in the tailoring trade in the East End. We had to stand in the centre of the hall, closely packed. The solo singer was Madame Galli-Curci, the best known of the opera singers of her time. At the end of each performance, especially the orchestral items, it seemed to me the audience clapped for as long as the performance had taken. I was sure I was never to become quite so fanatical. At the end we went to the Corner House at Piccadilly for tea where there was always an orchestra in attendance. Another entertainment I went to with Les was the Empire Exhibition at Wembley where we went on the giant racer, the equivalent of the modern big dipper. We sat two abreast, and there was a safety bar, which was pressed back against our midriffs after getting in. Leslie wore a bowler hat which he was advised to remove for the ride. He put this between his knees and, when we got off, there was the flattest bowler hat I have ever seen. It could never have looked as good afterwards. We both had very sore elbows, caused by holding on to the rail in front and rubbing them against the press bar when going down the steep dips and up the other side, at speeds which were said to be near 80mph. There were many other amusements, and it was probably the biggest collection I had ever seen at that time. Each country of

the Empire had its own pavilion, and I found those connected with farming very interesting, like the Canadian and Australian. As for the cinema, I was taken to see 'The Gold Rush', with Charlie Chaplin, at the Capitol, and 'The Iron Horse', dealing with the building of the railroad across the USA, at the Haymarket. We also attended the local cinema at Stoke Newington. One Sunday morning we went to Petticoat Lane to the open-air market, where it was said they pinched your watch at one end and sold it back to you at the other. Tottenham Hotspur was the local football team, and I went to see them play at White Hart Lane once or twice. One Sunday afternoon we went to Hampstead Heath and Parliament Hill Fields, and on another, to Hyde Park. It was at this time that I first met ice cream wrapped up in paper, tuppence a time. This was the same as the 'stop me and buy one' boys were later to sell in towns from box tricycles.

On looking out of the office window it was possible to see the tall Liberty building in Regent Street. Renovations must have been taking place as there was a big crane mounted on the roof and, about once a week, I saw a man climb right to the top of the jib which was at about 60 degrees. It was as if he was climbing a ladder using one hand to grip and carrying an oil can in the other. It was said his job was to lubricate the pulley wheel at the top. He must have been well over 150 feet up. I couldn't have done that although I could climb trees (and fall out).

Back in the office the circular letter scheme went ahead, and I discovered the method of selecting the recipients was by obtaining a list from various hospitals of their friends and patrons. Bridgwater Hospital was included, and I addressed many letters to villages I knew well. As time went on it became apparent to me, judging by the mail received, that the response was practically nil and, although I wasn't informed, I wondered how long the job would last. I think the adult whose name escapes me was the first to go. Then an event occurred which I imagine brought about the end. Ralph H and Eric P attended a rugby match at Twickenham, probably in October, and Ralph had the misfortune to be arrested for being drunk in charge of the Citroen. He was obviously bailed as he turned up at the office as usual on the following Monday morning. Eric told me the story, and I think he must have prompted me to write home. The upshot was that Mum arrived at Waterloo where I met her, and she had brother Jim with her. I was surprised to hear him talk but I cannot now think why as he was nearly three. I believe Mum stayed a day or two, and then we all went back to Shapwick. If it had been the most successful office in London I am sure I would not have stuck it as I was certainly not cut out to be an indoor type. The following day I was back in the big field pulling mangolds. I didn't like this either but the air was fresh. It was later learned that Ralph H got a month inside for the drink charge. I thought that a bit steep as he had no previous convictions to my knowledge, apart from the gun licence offence. No more was heard of him for two or three years when a report appeared in one of the daily newspapers that an Englishman named Ralph Hancock, FRHS, [1] had won an award for designing a garden on the top of one of New York's skyscrapers, and I think it was the Empire State Building. [2] This was followed later by the publication of a book, 'When I Build a Garden' by Ralph Hancock, FRHS. [3] That was the last I ever heard of him but he was an example of the fact that an enterprising man couldn't be kept down. He must have got the FRHS after I had left his office. [4] I never again heard of Eric Pittard who used to tell me he was related to the Yeovil family of the same name, engaged in the glove manufacturing business. He invited me to his home once, down Brixton way, on a Sunday, and I was surprised that lunch was not ready until 3pm. That was quite usual in most London homes, but not with Aunt Rose. The time from noon till lunch was spent in the pub by the menfolk, and I remember drinking Hoare's Toby ale with Eric but I couldn't keep pace with him. It was in November that I left London, and my total stay did not exceed 12 weeks.

1. Fellow of the Royal Horticultural Society.
2. It was the Rockefeller Centre.
3. 'When I Make a Garden' was first published in 1935.
4. This happened in 1926 and the following year he created gardens for Queen Victoria's daughter, Princess Victoria – a far cry from catching rabbits and shooting rooks in Shapwick.

WESTON: Family outing (Mabel, Charlie, Fred and Jim), 1931.

FRED'S MEMOIR:

BACK IN SHAPWICK
AND A FINAL FAREWELL

Within a couple of weeks of my return home, Dad bought a second-hand 1916 Ford Model 'T' four-seater open tourer, with hood and side curtains attached, from a garage in Wembdon Road, Bridgwater, for £25. The chief rival to the Model 'T' was the American General Motors Chevrolet of 22hp. It had the great advantage of a three-speed gearbox but cost more. The Model 'T' easily outsold it, but the Chevrolet was the better performer. Ford didn't change to a three-speed gearbox until about 1928.

I obtained a driving licence from Taunton and was sent to fetch the car. I said I could drive but the only experience I had had was the 200-yard trip in Ralph Hancock's Citroen. The boss said that he had better take me out as the Ford's gears were quite different from any other. I sat behind the wheel, and he gave the instructions. Off we went in the direction of Minehead, and when we had passed through Nether Stowey he said he was quite satisfied. Back we went to Bridgwater, where I dropped him, and then home I went on my own. In the 30-odd miles I had driven I don't recall meeting more than half-a-dozen other cars. I took the sharp right-hand corner into the yard in top gear and much too fast. I stopped in time so no damage was done but I always engaged low gear thereafter. There were only two forward speeds and a reverse. There was no clutch. There were three foot pedals, and the left operated both gears. When coming to a halt the handbrake was applied and this automatically pulled the left pedal back into neutral. The engine was switched on and started by turning the handle. Starter motors were yet to come. To start off, the pedal would be held in its neutral position by the left foot and the handbrake released. The pedal was then depressed, and this engaged low gear which was a band being tightened around a revolving drum, thus turning the rear wheels. There was no accelerator pedal, and the engine speed was governed by a throttle lever fixed to the steering column below the steering wheel. When near maximum speed had been reached the left foot was removed, and the pedal sprang back into top gear. This was a very jerky ride until top gear got up to 15 or 20 miles per hour, as the difference between the two gear ratios was very wide. A modern comparison would be to change from first or second gear into top, missing out the intermediaries. The

low had to be low enough to get up the steepest hill encountered and the top sufficiently high to make a motorcar fast enough to be worthwhile. Reversing was done by holding the forward pedal in neutral position with the foot (handbrake off of course) and depressing the centre pedal with the right. Skilful drivers, and I think I became one of them, could go back and forth in a Model 'T' much faster than any present day car. This was well demonstrated later on in some of the Laurel and Hardy films. The lighting consisted of oil-burning side and tail lamps which very often blew out in high wind. Many matches were used in getting them re-lit. The headlamps were acetylene, and the container for the carbide and water was mounted on the offside running board. The rubber connecting pipes were prone to becoming blocked with water but when functioning well the light was very good; there was no dipping system. Extreme cold presented a problem when the water for the carbide froze up but this didn't often occur. The ignition system on the standard Model 'T' was generated by the flywheel (starter column I think it was known as), but ours had been converted to magneto, a Sims Bosch, which was driven by an open chain. The advantage was said to be that backfiring when starting could be eliminated. There was an advance/retard lever for both systems on the steering column opposite the throttle lever, but even when fully retarded the Ford system still backfired (or 'kicked', as it was known). If the engine would start with a 'pull up' it wasn't so bad but if it had to be 'swung' (the handle turned full circle continuously) the trouble started when the downward stroke commenced. If you were strong enough to get a fast first upward swing you could overcome the 'kick' on the downward. The advice always was to grasp the handle in a monkey grip, that is the thumb over the top in line with the fingers, otherwise a dislocated thumb could result with any 'kick'. Even with this precaution broken arms and wrists still occurred; the Bristol hospitals were said to handle an average of two per day, and they were christened 'Ford arms'. I have seen the starting handle fly backwards and revolve like an aeroplane propeller. The fractures occurred when the hand was not withdrawn fast enough and the handle hit the operator on or near the wrist. We had no such problem with our magneto. The headlights on the normal Model 'T' were electric and driven off the flywheel like the ignition. But when the engine slowed down, the lights dimmed, and it was only at reasonable speeds that the light was good. When you came to a corner and dropped the engine revs the lights dimmed just when required most. The index number of ours was AJ 2901 (Yorkshire), and the car probably started life in the army. The horsepower rating was 23, and the road fund tax at the time £1 per hp so this was £23 per year.

We were told we could obtain hackney carriage rate at £12 per year if we did hire work, which was the intention as there was an opening at Shapwick, especially catching or meeting trains at Shapwick Station. The standard charge was sixpence per mile for the total distance, and this brought in two and sixpence to the station. There was little demand, however, so it was not likely to provide a living by itself. Miss Hilborne, the new Headmistress, and her colleague were the best customers, and she always gave me three and sixpence for the station trip. By the time I had stopped whatever I was doing on the farm to go to the station, at least an hour would have elapsed until I got back, and all for two and sixpence. The road fund licence on the car when we bought it expired on the following 31st December and, upon application for the hackney carriage licence we had been told about, the licensing authority at Taunton turned it down on the grounds that the car was not used primarily for hire work. And so we had to pay the full rate of £23. The present day equivalent would be about £700.

Petrol was not more than two shillings per gallon, and this was delivered weekly by motor lorry from the Pratts (now Esso) depot at Wells. It came in two-gallon cans with an initial deposit of four shillings on each can so that at the next call the empties would be exchanged for full ones. We bought four gallons per week on average, and some of this went into the Amanco engine.

During the spring and summer of 1926 the demand increased, and I occasionally took up to four people to Weston Super Mare for the day for £1. The professionals charged waiting time but there wouldn't have been much trade if we had done this. For Bristol it was £1 10s 0d, but there weren't many customers. Dad continued to supply the shop in Church Road with apples, eggs, etc, and I drove the Model 'T' heavily laden several times, either via Wells or Axbridge.[1] The hill out of Wells and Redhill always required low gear, at not much more than 6/8 mph, and I got a warmed-up left foot by the time the top was reached. Some of the return trips were made in darkness and, on one occasion, there was fog from Bedminster Down until I was clear of the Mendips. The windscreen was two-piece with the top half hinged so that it could be folded down. Windscreen wipers still had to be invented

and, in poor conditions, I turned the screen down for an unobstructed view but got very cold as a result. Normal time for the journey was one and a half hours but foggy conditions doubled it. Another hazard in the winter was floodwater and, from the bottom of Mudgeley Hill to Westhay, the road was often covered in up to six inches. The only guide was the willow trees set well back from the road on both sides, and it wasn't easy to keep to the centre of the road, especially at night. Fatalities had occurred in the past, even with horse-drawn vehicles. The hood and side curtains were only used in rain and provided reasonable protection. The hood folded down like a pram hood when not in use and could be erected in a minute or so. The side curtains, canvas with celluloid windows, took a bit longer and were fixed with turn buttons.

In the summer of 1926 Edgar Godwin and his wife from near Chicago, USA, came to stay at Shapwick on holiday. Edgar was the brother of Johnnie and Albert and he had been in the States since the early 1900s. He proved a very good customer, and I took him all over Somerset to visit relatives and friends. He called me 'Freddie' and always provided all the cigarettes (Wills Gold Flake) that I could smoke during the day. One of his brothers or his wife's relatives came along to fill the four passenger seats, three in the back and Edgar up front with me. On a visit to Cheddar caves I was coming up to the car park on my right with the bright sun in my eyes. I honestly did not see the policeman or the stop signal he had given me and I turned into the car park. He accepted my explanation but I got a good ticking off. The last trip I did was to take Edgar and his wife to the station for their return to the USA, a tearful occasion for Mrs Godwin as she felt sure she would never see Shapwick again. But they came again about two years later, and I drove them a few times in the Citroen we had then. It was decided, when the hackney carriage licence was refused, that we would change to a car of smaller horsepower when finances allowed. At this time the car salesmen used to call at the farms to promote their products, and one such was Frank Bishop from the Ford agent at Taunton. When he knew a new Ford (less than £200) was out of the question he sent along one of his pals with a 1923 model Citroen 11.4hp open tourer with an English body, index number XN 440 (London), which was taxed at £12 per year and capable of carrying as many passengers as the Model 'T'. This was about the autumn of 1926. I think they wanted £125 and would allow £10 for the Ford, the balance on hire purchase. The deal was struck, and the advantage of electric lighting all round, lower body with more comfort, plus a three-speed gearbox, soon became apparent. The hood was the same style but the sides were protected with side screens which fitted into the doors and were not

1. Apparently my grandfather took over this shop, which was in Redfield, Bristol, as the result of a bad debt. My grandmother ran it, so she must have been living there, but I don't know how long this arrangement lasted.

hampered by any canvas surround. The all-round visibility was so much better, and so was the mpg. There was no speedometer or mileometer on this or the Model 'T' so that miles per hour could only be guessed, as was the distance travelled, aided by the signposts. My charge was sometimes disputed over the miles, and 'countrymen's' miles differed from reality. I got in the habit of agreeing the price beforehand in some cases, and there was the occasional customer who said he would 'settle up with Dad later on'. I always got paid eventually, and once or twice in kind. An oak roll-top desk came in lieu of 30 shillings for taking Mr Golladge of the King William pub, Catcott, to Yatton or Nailsea.

There was a 'Johnny Fortnight' or travelling tailor/ clothier named Jacobs who lived at Weston. In the early days he used a bicycle but soon after we got the Citroen he said he was going to give up cycling. He offered me the job of picking him up at the Street Inn every other Saturday and conveying him through the villages to make his calls, finishing up at Bridgwater. He could take more than his fair share of beer etc and, on arriving at the Street Inn, my first task was to drink the half-pint he had ordered for me. There would be another half-pint or so at Chilton Polden and, in his case, a whisky or two. I never took more than I thought I could manage until there was a special celebration at the Street Inn with Mr Jacobs, the landlord Arthur Love and one of their other pals. I made the fourth, and out came a bottle of champagne, shared between the four. The other three paid for the bottle, equally shared, but I couldn't pay as I didn't have any money. In any case we had all had too much, and it was soon obvious to Mr Jacobs, who could carry it much better than I could, that I was not really capable of driving, and he decided to miss out the villages. When we got to the turning to Edington, off the A 39, he told me to pull onto the grass verge and have a sleep. When I woke, some hours later, I was quite alone but had obviously had a visitor as big stones had been piled on the running boards. I never found out who did it. I was more cautious afterwards, and still continued to drive Mr J for a while.

After Uncle Bill's arrival in June 1927, we did not employ any outside labour, and Clifford took over the cows while Uncle Bill and I did the ploughing, harvesting, etc, or whatever involved the horses. I continued the hire work with the Citroen, mostly meeting or taking passengers to Shapwick Station. In the summer there was the occasional trip to Burnham, Weston or Minehead, and a few times to the Bristol General Hospital with patients. At sixpence per mile and no waiting time charged, this was not a paying proposition. For instance, I got £1 for a whole day to Weston. The wear and tear and running costs of the car must have been at least 15 shillings. On looking back it seems obvious that we must have been getting deeper and deeper into debt, and in January 1929

Uncle Jack secured a contract to build six council houses at Lympsham, near Weston Super Mare – three pairs. This was about 20 miles from Shapwick via Bawdrip, and I agreed to pick up Uncle Jack and three others at Bawdrip before 8am, Monday to Saturday, and drive them to the site, work there all day myself and return home, for £4.10s 0d per week. I was regarded as an apprentice carpenter and started like all the rest by digging the foundations. It was hard work but I got used to it, and by July the outside structure of all the three blocks was complete. To finish meant a drop in the labour force, and as the car was no longer needed I bought a second-hand AJS 350cc overhead-valve motorcycle from Taylor's, London, without even seeing it beforehand, for £27. I picked it up from the train at Shapwick Station, and it started first time. I used this to pick up Reg March, my cousin, or sometimes Uncle Fred, to go to Lympsham, and this went on until about September when the job was completed. Uncle Jack had a Matchless motorcycle which his son Clifford rode right from the start, but when the car was taken off he rode pillion to Clifford. Cliff used to like to lead the way, but I could always get to the top of Puriton Hill first as I had more revs than his Matchless 500cc side valve. We were coming home once and Cliff was in the lead, as usual, with cousin Ralph Willcocks on the pillion. Ralph was on holiday at Bawdrip (from London) at the time. We were taking the Edithmead, Bason Bridge, Woolavington road which meant turning left from the A38 north of Highbridge. Cliff was taking the corner much too fast when the inevitable happened and both were thrown off. Ralph was yelling with pain whereas Cliff was quite unhurt, and muttered something about stopping yelling and getting on the back (pillion). I mentioned this to Ralph in about 1972, and he said he still had the scars. I had Uncle Fred on the back a few times, and he was always very nervous and kept telling me to go steady. Actually I always did and never drove with the throttle wide open. I was approaching the crossroads at Brent Knowle on the homeward journey with Uncle Fred aboard, nagging me as usual, when a car was seen coming up to the junction from Rooksbridge, thus crossing our path. I had seen it and was quite prepared to stop if necessary, but Uncle Fred kept shouting 'Look out!', at the same time wriggling farther and farther back on the pillion, which meant I was gradually losing control and I had to stop. Although I was always reassuring him that I had no intention of committing suicide I don't think he ever changed. He must have been over 40 years of age at the time, and I can well understand his nervousness now. I don't think he ever rode behind Clifford.

During the time I drove the Citroen, about 40 miles a day, six days a week, over six months or more, it never broke down and must have done a few thousand miles all told. Neither did the AJS ever conk out but I had a near miss on one occasion when I got an electric shock from the plug

WINCANTON: Fred on joining the AA in 1930.

lead when it was raining. I finished up halfway down the bank and almost in the water in a ditch near the Fox and Goose Inn. I managed to pull the bike out and get home safely.

While I was at Lympsham – January to September 1929 – Uncle Bill and my brother Clifford kept the farm going, and there did not appear to be any place for me. There was a chap called Reg Franks living in Shapwick, who was known for his ability to sell peat, and somehow or other Dad and Uncle Walter (at the Albion) were persuaded to join up and buy a second-hand Fiat one-ton lorry, which had belonged to coal merchants Buckton of Brent Knowle. It was, I believe, a First World War leftover, and the rim of the steering wheel was iron. The idea was to load this with 1,000 pieces of burning peat from near Shapwick Station, cost 12 shillings, and hawk it wherever Reg Franks thought fit, selling door to door in small lots but preferably the whole load at one drop. I drove the lorry and travelled wider than I had ever done

before, chiefly within Somerset, but on one occasion we arrived at Chipping Sodbury in Gloucestershire with the full load still on. Reg called at a pub to enquire about a probable customer, and we ended up selling the load in a big house which I feel sure was Dodington or Dyrham. He had a liking for big houses, and his ploy was that he was en route to somewhere a few miles farther on but did not want to continue as the lorry was developing trouble. He was supposed to hand all the takings to Uncle Walter and be paid his agreed commission, but I am sure he never did so, and I caught him out quite a few times. By the time we got home most days he was half drunk as he never failed to call at a pub and drink whisky when he had had a good sale. He was quite a character and had been in all sorts of jobs prior to this, including a few trips with the Cunard line to New York. He got a paternity order against him by a girl near Watchet, which prompted him to bolt and he made for South Wales where he worked at the pithead. A policeman turned up one day and said to him that he had a warrant for Reg Franks and did he know where he was. Reg said he did and told the PC where to look whereupon he (Reg) scarpered. He sang his way in the streets (including Gloucester), eventually reaching Southampton, where he got a job on commission selling Singer sewing machines in the New Forest. He was told there was pay and commission for the first week but commission only thereafter. He lugged the sewing machine around for one week and made not one sale. The end of the second week produced the same result so he told the boss he had come to the conclusion Singer sewing machines were like bumholes (not his exact words) as every bugger had one. He eventually returned to Shapwick and married a Walton girl by whom there were some children. I tried to act as peacemaker once when she left him. It didn't work then but I think they eventually got back together. He died early in life in the 1930s, I think, after I had left Shapwick.

By the end of 1929 I could see I had no future with Reg Franks and, after having been turned down by the Somerset Police for lack of half an inch round the chest and by the Metropolitan Police for lack of 2lb, I applied to the AA. In early 1930 I had an interview at Bridgwater and, in March, I got the job of patrolling the road, on a pedal cycle, between Wincanton and Ilchester, via Sparkford, a distance of about 12 and a half miles, up and down hills most of the way. I lodged with Mrs White at 22 Mill Street, Wincanton, to whom I paid 35 shillings per week, whilst my pay was 45 shillings. She already had two male lodgers, and we shared one large bedroom, each of us with a single bed. Jack Warner was one of them, himself an ex AA patrolman and he came from Tewkesbury. His people ran coaches there. I started at 9am daily and worked until lighting-up time, which meant the day's work gradually got longer until it reached 8pm, and that was finishing time right through the summer, except Sunday when I started at 10am and finished at

Right - WINCANTON: 20 and 22 Mill Street, 1985.

Bottom - ILCHESTER: Fred on the Triumph motorcycle combination, summer 1930.

9pm. There was only one day off per week, and that was Tuesday so there was never a weekend. I always went home after duty on Monday and returned on Wednesday morning using my AJS. I must have left Shapwick soon after 7am in order to be on the road by 9am. I used to make the journey from Wincanton to Ilchester and back twice daily, and that meant I had cycled 50-plus miles. At Ilchester I met the AA patrol on traffic duty at the junction where my road met the Fosse Way from Shepton Mallet. In the afternoon I relieved him while he had his tea, and this was my first experience of traffic duty. After about six weeks cycling I was given a Triumph motorcycle combination, as the AA then used, and this made life much easier. I was supposed to cover more ground but didn't unless I got diverted to a breakdown. There was a sergeant, an inspector and a chief inspector, and their job was to travel the route at frequent intervals to see what the privates like me were up to. I carried a diary in which I had to record the times and places as I reached them, and the visits by the senior officers. There was commission for all new members enrolled, about six shillings for a car, and I think I got about eight during my time. I made far more from tips by assisting members who had broken down or run out of petrol. The most common cause of breakdown was blockage of the carburettor jets, mostly on Morris Cowleys, which were the most common cars of the time. I reckoned to put these right within 15 minutes, and the tips ranged from nothing to five shillings. Anything too big to handle was sent to the nearest AA-appointed garage, and that brought in a few more shillings from the proprietor. My motorcycle combination was kept at Budgen's garage in Wincanton and, on one occasion when starting off in the morning, my rear wheel shot a stone straight through a shop window, or so I was told by the shopkeeper at the end of the day. I reported no knowledge of the incident and I don't know how it was resolved.

Bicknoller, 1979.

Stogumber, 1979.

PART 2 - A FAMILY HISTORY:

APPLEDORE or JENNINGS?

I'm not sure whether my father had reached the point where he intended to stop, as it does seem a rather abrupt ending. He had certainly fulfilled what I asked him to do and he might just have run out of steam. There is another explanation, for it was whilst Dad was writing his memoir that my brother-in-law, Michael Callister, mentioned that his great-grandfather had died in an accident in the 1890s and he was now engaged in trying to find out more about the circumstances. Dad was immediately interested, as he knew that his own grandfather had been killed around the same time. Armed with the little information which my dad was able to supply, Michael went to the newspaper library at Colindale and managed to trace accounts of the death in two contemporary editions. What followed was something of a Pandora's Box and eventually led to the discovery of information which my father would probably have preferred not to know. Once you embark upon the ancestral trail, it is hard to let go. This was clearly so in my dad's case and probably accounts for the sudden ending of his memoir as his attention had been diverted elsewhere.

After his death, I found documents relating to the family tree, along with lots of correspondence he had entered into with various organisations and individuals in his quest to find answers to so many questions. There were copies of official documents and of letters he had written, the replies he received, some photographs and summaries of the information Michael and he had uncovered so far. Everything was carefully filed away in a box and in large envelopes, all very clearly labelled. It was so typical of my dad, who was very methodical and meticulous. On finding this material, it struck me that it would be a great pity to waste it so I decided to take up the challenge and finish what Dad and Michael had started years before.

My original intention was to try to document the lives of my great-grandfather and grandfather but once I began delving into the records I was presented with some information which I just couldn't ignore. As a result, my search was extended into the eighteenth century where I discovered who my great-great-great grandparents were, but with only scant detail of their lives. So this is where my contribution to the tale begins. I have deliberately avoided placing great emphasis on how I carried out the research, including the order in which the information came to light, as I feel it would detract from the narrative. Instead I have tried to present a picture of events as they happened at the time, beginning in the 1800s and ending

in the twentieth century. It is, in fact, the reverse of the accepted genealogical methodology, in which you are advised to work backwards through time to build up a family tree. Where appropriate, I indicate the sources and location of the records involved.

Along the way I encountered many mysteries and surprises, not least of which was the fact that some of my ancestors were using an alias. The first indication of this appeared in Dr Campbell's Index, housed in Somerset Record Office and an invaluable tool for genealogists interested in the West Somerset area. The doctor listed all the baptismal and marriage entries from the old records according to surname and parish. Whilst examining those relating to Jennings, I came across some marked 'als Appledore', als being the abbreviation for alias. This called for some clarification as it kept on cropping up in so many of the early records.

To find out more meant trawling through copies of some very old documents and it looked as though the earliest mention of 'Appledore' was the baptism in 1584 of 'Ellis Apulder, son of John Apulder' in Milverton. Further entries showed the names Jennings and Appledore were being used interchangeably, some written as 'Jennings alias Appledore' and others as 'Appledore alias Jennings'. Today we often associate the use of an alias with fraud, but this was not the case long ago. It was quite a common practice during the sixteenth and seventeenth centuries but was gradually phased out during the eighteenth century, although not entirely by one member of the Jennings family, as we shall see. So why did it happen? I could offer no definitive explanation at first, despite extensive research into the use of aliases. The reasons I came across were unlikely to apply to the Jennings/Appledore case, but then Stephen Jennings, a distant relative, mentioned that he'd found two 'men-at-arms', John Appledore and William Appledore, on a website about medieval soldiers. This information seemed to place the name firmly in Devon during the fourteenth century.

Bearing this in mind, I now suspect that Appledore was the name the ancestors were using initially, before the use of surnames became widespread. Historians believe that most people in England didn't acquire an hereditary surname until around the end of the fourteenth century. Before this, a few male first names were becoming very common so if, for example, there was more than one 'John' in a village or hamlet, some other means of identifying them became necessary. It is impossible to tell if this is what happened in the case of Appledore, but it is the most likely explanation I have encountered. Since Appledore is a place name and not a recognised surname it could be the reason why the family eventually adopted Jennings in preference to Appledore. Many surnames were derived from diminutives of first names, which is how Jennings developed. Researching the origin of our surname, I found there was general agreement that Jennings is a patronymic (a name taken from a father's first name) from the Middle English given name Janyn or Jenyn, which is a diminutive of John.

There is no doubt that the surname Jennings underwent some transformation over the centuries, before arriving at the current version. A glance at the old records reveals this was not a swift or consistent process, even allowing for local pronunciation and the scribes' attempts at recording what they heard. I've come across *'Jennins, Jenings, Jenins, Jenninges, Ginnings and Gennynge'* to name but a few (and not in chronological order). These are matched by a variety of spellings of Appledore: *'Apulder, Apeldor, Apoldoar, Apaldor'* and those are just some of the ones I was able to decipher. Jennings, then, prevailed, much to the annoyance of my mother who complained that it was difficult to write because of 'all those bloody *ns*'.

I cannot account for the frequent use of both names with one or the other being written as the alias, unless it was to distinguish a particular branch of the family. The entries referring to Jennings/Appledore in the records are so numerous that I can only conclude that our ancestors were extremely prolific, and that, along with the extensive use of the same first names down through the generations, some additional means of identification could have been required.

It seems safe to assume that the family's earliest traceable origins lie in Devon, where there are several locations which go by the name of Appledore. Apart from the well-known coastal resort, there is a couple of hamlets and farmsteads. The one near Burlescombe is so close to the Somerset border that I thought this would be the most likely spot but no evidence was found to support it. There was a small cluster of people named Jennings/Appledore living in Cruwys Morchard during the seventeenth century, which is a parish lying to the southwest of Tiverton. Although not very close to the boundary with Somerset, it might well have been of some relevance and confirms the Devon connection. There was some movement of families as marriages took place between people of different parishes, so perhaps this explains the eventual migration of some members of the family into Somerset.

When I picked up the story, the ancestors in my direct line were well and truly established in West Somerset, most notably in Bicknoller and Stogumber, two beautiful villages nestling among the Quantock Hills. This location was the first in the country to be designated an area of outstanding natural beauty, and with good reason. And so, set within the confines of just a few neighbouring parishes, the Jennings family tale unfolds.

PART 2 - A FAMILY HISTORY:

JAMES and HARRIET JENNINGS

My great-great-great grandfather Thomas was born in about 1741 so when he married Sarah Welch on 18th January 1772 in Sampford Brett he was approximately 31 years of age. She was younger, by about ten years, making her 21 or so. In the marriage register, Thomas was recorded as *'Thomas Appledore alias Jennings of the Parish of Bicknoller, Bachelor'*. [1] Both he and Sarah were unable to sign their names but each made their mark. Sometime after their marriage, they had taken up residence in Stogumber, where their first child, John (i.e. live birth), was baptised on 20th February 1774. The following eight children were also baptised there:

Robert, 26th May 1776
Thomas, 30th November 1777
Sarah, 2nd January 1780
Francis, 7th August 1785
Mary, 18th February 1787
Elizabeth, 23rd August 1789
Martha, 2nd September 1792
James, 7th May 1796

This might not have been the entire brood as there is a couple of long gaps where Sarah might have miscarried or had a stillborn baby which, in the days before birth certificates were required by law, would have gone unreported. Deaths of stillborn infants didn't actually have to be notified until 1874, although live births were registered from 1837.

Of Thomas and Sarah's nine children, the youngest, baptised James Appledore, (there was no mention of Jennings in the baptismal register) was of the most interest to me as he was my great-great-grandfather. It was the uncovering of some quite disturbing information about this man that persuaded me he should feature in my account. For a long time I had been aware that he had married Harriet Coles on 8th November 1832 as Michael had discovered this in the 1970s. Harriet was the illegitimate daughter of Mary Coles and she was baptised in Crowcombe on 15th February 1807. At the time of their marriage she was nearly 26 and James was about 36. They were married in Williton Chapel in the parish of St Decuman and the marriage register [2] reads as follows:

James Jennings   *of_____Parish and* Harriet Coles

both of (sic) *of* this *Parish were married in this* Chapel *by* Banns *with Consent of_____ this* eighth *Day of* November *in the Year One thousand eight hundred and* thirty two

By me Charles Poole Incumbent
This Marriage was solemnized between us { Jas Jennings

Harriet Coles
In the Presence of { _____ Henry Chidgey
                          _____ John Hale
No. 22

This shows that they were both living in Williton but for how long prior to the marriage is not known. Weddings usually took place in the bride's parish but she had to be resident there for just four weeks beforehand. If a betrothed couple lived in different parishes, banns were called in each parish and each set had to be paid for. Thus it was cheaper for them to reside in the same parish whilst the banns were being called, and so James might have gone to stay in Williton to save on the expense.

The register records that the marriage was conducted by one *'Charles Poole, Incumbent'* and was witnessed by Henry Chidgey who, having married James's sister Martha in 1819 at St Decuman's (Dr Campbell's Index), was his brother-in-law. The second witness, John Hale, might have been an official of the church as his signature appears on the following two entries in the register. All the parties involved signed their names although Harriet's version of her first name looks pretty dodgy so perhaps she'd been practising specifically for this occasion.

It seems that 'the happy couple' continued to live in Williton or nearby as their first child, Martha, was baptised in the parish of St Decuman on 26th January 1833. Yes, the timing struck me immediately – this was indeed 'a shotgun marriage' which must have been very obvious at the wedding ceremony. They had left it so late, even allowing for the calling of the banns, that poor Harriet must have wondered whether she was about to suffer the same fate as her mother and literally be left holding the baby. James, however, decided to do 'the right thing' and the child was just about born in wedlock. I think it shows there must have been a certain reluctance on his part, in view of what was to follow.

1. Somerset Record Office Ref: D/P/5 s b 2/1/5.
2. D/P/will 2/1/3.

James and Harriet went on to have three more children: John, born about 1835, Mary, about 1836, and James, who was born on 1st March 1839. Sometime between the births of Martha and John, the family moved to Bicknoller. (The census of 1851 confirms that the three younger children were all born there.) A birth certificate was only available for James, the youngest child, as the civil registration system was not introduced into England and Wales until 1st July 1837. From then onwards, it was compulsory to notify all live births, marriages and deaths to the local registrar. The information on the certificate shows that young James was born in Kingswood in Bicknoller and that his father was a carpenter. His mother registered the birth on 7th April 1839, which fell within the statutory six weeks allowed.

The four children were baptised in Bicknoller on 29th November 1840. According to the baptismal register,[3] Martha was then aged eight, John was six, Mary was five and James's age was recorded as two years although he wasn't quite. The parents were 'James and Harriett (sic) Jennings' and the family was living in Yard. Although James's birth certificate gave Kingswood in Bicknoller as the place where he was born, Yard is so close to Kingswood that they might well have still been living in the same cottage.

Was John Llewellin, who was the officiating minister, aware that Martha had already been baptised in 1833? It seems rather strange for a child to undergo a second baptism so was there a good reason for it? At first, I thought it might not have been the same child as it was not uncommon for parents to name another child after a dead sibling, but Martha appears to have been one and the same from her age recorded in the Bicknoller baptismal register and according to the censuses of 1841 and 1851.

What was even more odd was that the youngest child's name was written as 'Jane' in the register. Clearly, why this happened can only be guessed at and several possibilities spring to mind. Notes taken of the children's details prior to the baptism might have been badly written so that 'James' looked like 'Jane'. Perhaps the scribe had a hearing loss, and as the little boy was just under two years old it could have been impossible to distinguish boy from girl by its outward appearance. Or could it be that just a drop too much communion wine had been imbibed that day? It is very unlikely that either parent would have been able to point out the error and so it was that James went down in perpetuity baptised as a girl.

During the following year, on 6th June 1841, a census was taken of the population and, for the first time, contained individuals' details rather than just the simple headcount of the previous ones of 1801 to 1831. Although quite basic, it provided enough information to prompt the need for some further research. The Bicknoller census confirmed that the family was living in Yard, at least Harriet and the four children were. Her age was given as 30, which was consistent with the practice of 'rounding down', as the enumerators had been instructed to do – she was actually about 34 years old. It stated that she was working as an agricultural labourer even though she had four children under the age of ten. It is also possible that Martha was working too as against her name on the form was written 'labourer' but this might have been crossed out. But the biggest surprise was that there was no mention of husband James, so was he away working on that occasion or could he have died? Neither of the above, in fact, although the latter seemed to be the case from the 1851 census where Harriet was described as a widow. By then she was working as a washerwoman. So what had happened to James? It was time to contact Somerset Record Office to find out if there was any record of his whereabouts, or when and where he had died. There was no mention of him in the National Burial Index between 1839 and 1851 and no sign of a will. He did not feature in the Calendars of Prisoners from 1839 to 1842, but there were references to the family in the Settlement Index[4]. Philip Hocking, the researcher, sent me copies of the relevant documents, which proved to be 'historical gold'. This set of papers provided so much information about the family and, without them, that would have been the end of the story as far as my great-great-grandfather was concerned. A significant event in the family's history would have passed unnoticed as well as all the details it brought in its wake. Before I examined the contents of the settlement papers, I needed a better understanding of how the poor were dealt with in the days before the advent of the welfare state, because this is what I was now confronted with – my ancestors weren't just poor, they were destitute.

In medieval times, the poor had been cared for by the church, with the distribution of alms carried out by the religious houses. This must have been a somewhat haphazard process which was not improved with the dissolution of the monasteries by Henry the Eighth. It was then decreed that they should become the responsibility of each parish, to be financed by voluntary donations which, as might be expected, did not deliver sufficient funds. Eventually, in an attempt to formalise the provision of poor relief, the Poor Law Act was introduced in 1601 during the reign of Elizabeth the First, whereby taxes were raised from parishioners specifically to fund it. The Act decreed that a pauper could only claim poor relief in his or her parish of 'legal settlement', an entitlement which was granted after settling in that parish for at least one month.

3. Ref: D/P/bic 2/1/8.
4. Ref: DD/SAS/SX 39, folder 9, numbers 10, 27, 28, 32 and 62, D/P/bic 13/3/63.

It comes as no surprise to know that this system was soon open to abuse as it encouraged people not to seek work, but to depend on poor relief in the parish of their choice once they had lived there for upwards of a month. This resulted in a very large burden on taxpaying parishioners, so in 1662 the Act was replaced by the Poor Relief Act, which laid down more stringent criteria for acquiring a 'legal settlement'. Known as the Settlement Act, its aim was to ensure that only those legally settled in a parish would be eligible to claim poor relief within that parish. Thus it was essential to establish where your place of legal settlement was under the new act in case you became unable to support yourself and your family. It seems to have been quite a complex process as it wasn't necessarily the place where you were born or baptised: for example, a woman acquired the right to her husband's legal settlement on her marriage, and children of seven or under from the marriage also took their father's right to a settlement. This led to many disputes between parishes about whose responsibility it was to maintain a pauper family because of the financial cost to the taxpayers. Where no agreement was reached between parishes, the case was referred to the Justices of the Peace who would decide the outcome.

The system was changed again by the Poor Law Amendment Act of 1834 whereby Poor Law Unions were set up to administer poor relief – previously it had been dispensed by the vestry or parish council. A union consisted of a group of parishes, and was headed by a Board of Guardians who were elected by the ratepayers. The unions were then subdivided into districts, with a Relieving Officer who was responsible for doling out poor relief to those deemed eligible by the Overseers of the Poor, offices which date back to the sixteenth century. The nature of the relief also changed, from 'outdoor', which had been paid in cash or in kind, to 'indoor', which meant entry into the workhouse. However, outdoor relief continued to be paid to deserving cases such as widows with dependent children.

It was against this background that I began to study the settlement papers relating to the case of James and Harriet Jennings and their children. I have tried to piece together their story from the evidence contained in the papers, but it doesn't give the full picture and lots of questions remain unanswered. Nevertheless, there is much valuable information contained in the eight papers. Three are dated 26th July 1839, four are dated 1st August 1839 and just one 15th November 1839, so it is possible to arrange the events in chronological order [5]. Extracting exactly what happened necessarily entails a degree of speculation on my part but it is firmly based on the evidence given at the time.

Soon after their youngest child was born on 1st March 1839, it seems that James deserted the family, forcing Harriet to seek poor relief. On 26th July, David Howse, who was 'the Relieving Officer for the second District of the Williton Union', gave Harriet 'four shillings in money and four loaves of bread' as instructed by the Williton Board of Guardians. This action was contested by one of the overseers of the poor in Bicknoller, and the case was brought before one of Her Majesty's Justices of the Peace on the very same day. The Justice of the Peace was Thomas Cridland Luxton, a wealthy local landowner, and the complaining overseer was George Blake, who was a farmer. Blake testified that James Jennings, whom he knew, was 'a person able to maintain himself and his family by work and other means' but had left Bicknoller about three months earlier and 'has not since been there' thereby rendering Harriet and the four children 'chargeable to the parish of Bicknoller through his neglect to maintain them'.

Luxton issued what amounted to an arrest warrant for the return of James, appointing the same George Blake as his constable for the purpose of apprehending the runaway. This instruction was passed to the constable of the parish of Wembdon and 'to all others of her Majesty's officers of the Peace for the said County', so the hunt was on. Those charged with the task were exhorted to go about their business with the command 'Herein fail you not'. It would be James's opportunity 'to answer unto the said complaint, and to be further dealt withal according to Law'. Serious stuff indeed! And it was set to get even more so. As specific mention was made of Wembdon, which is near Bridgwater, it is possible that James had been sighted there and somebody had shopped him. The papers give no clue to how or where he was found, but he was brought back and appeared before two Justices of the Peace on 1st August 1839. As only five days had elapsed between the two dates given on the settlement papers, he couldn't have been very far away.

In order to determine his last place of legal settlement, he was examined under oath by the magistrates, TC Luxton and George Tripp. Having been absent for three months, he was said to be 'now residing in the Parish of Bicknoller' but there is no mention of his abode, so perhaps he might have been forced to return home. Those who deserted their families and went on the run, refusing to work, were classed as vagrants and could be convicted as such. Many ended up sleeping rough, in barns or out in the open, and there would have been no shortage of likely places around Bicknoller. There is nothing to suggest that such a fate befell James, who came from a large family and might have been offered temporary shelter by a relative.

5. Ref: D/P/bic 13/3/63.

His testimony, though quite revealing in some aspects, leaves the fundamental question of why he abandoned his family unanswered. The main concern of the Justices was to establish which parish was legally responsible for maintaining them, rather than why he refused to work and had neglected his dependants. Under oath, he began by stating: *'I have heard and believe that I was born in the Parish of Stogumber in the said County where my parents then resided and were legally settled as I have also heard and believe. I am now about forty two years old*[6]. *I was never apprenticed. When I was about sixteen years old I agreed to work for my brother Thomas Jennings who was a Carpenter then residing in Bicknoller aforesaid. He was to pay me two shillings a week and to teach me his trade to find me in meat, drink and lodging – except Sundays when I was to go home to my parents in Stogumber for my victuals*[7]. *No time was mentioned and there was no written agreement or Indenture. I worked for him accordingly for about three years in the parish of Bicknoller – except Sundays which I spent in Stogumber Parish with my Parents. I usually went home to them Saturday nights and returned to my work in Bicknoller Monday mornings. I then went and worked for my brother John Jennings in the Parish of Stogumber. He agreed to find me in everything and to teach me the 'joining and millwrighting'. No time was mentioned and there was no writing. I worked for him there for about four years. I have ever since worked at my trade as a journeyman and have not done any act to gain a settlement. About seven years ago I was married by bans* (sic) *in Williton Chapel to Harriet my present wife by whom I have four children all born in wedlock* [8] *named Martha aged about six years, John aged about four years, Mary aged about two years and James aged about half a year'.* He finished by saying that he and the family were now chargeable to the parish of Bicknoller.

I'll bet that final utterance endeared him to the Justices. Was he really telling them that he was entitled to poor relief when he wouldn't work? It seems that they were not prepared to accept his statement without further corroboration from another witness, his eldest brother, John, the millwright. To be fair to James, it was not uncommon for others to be interviewed on such occasions, often relatives of the examinee. John confirmed that James was born in the parish of Stogumber where their parents had been legally settled. He said that his father and mother were dead, stating, *'My father died four or five and twenty years ago* [9] *and my Mother about three years ago'.* [10] He went on to say that his parents had lived in a leasehold property in Stogumber, where his father had

died, and his mother had stayed there until the lease expired 14 or 15 years previously. John then continued: *'She never to my knowledge or belief gained a settlement elsewhere after her husband's death and about seven years ago the Parish officers of Stogumber obtained an order of Justices for my maintaining her which I did until her death about three years ago'.* How much reliance can be placed on any of the dates mentioned is questionable (e.g. there are discrepancies between the children's ages, although only slight), as people's memories are notoriously unreliable, even more so if you were unable to read and write or did not have access to a calendar or diary. But there are some revealing snippets of information in John's testimony to which I'll return later.

At this stage of the proceedings it wasn't looking good for Stogumber as John had confirmed that it was the parents' place of legal settlement, and therefore, by implication, that of their son James. The next move was made by the Justices who, having deliberated the case, delivered their verdict on the day of the hearing. They issued an order to the churchwardens and overseers of the poor in both Bicknoller and Stogumber, declaring that, as James and his family had acquired no legal settlement in Bicknoller, they were to be removed to Stogumber. They would then become chargeable to the latter parish. The order, in keeping with the other settlement papers, consisted of a statutory form which had to be completed by hand, presumably by a clerk on the instruction of the Justices. It concludes: *'WE do therefore require you the said Churchwardens and Overseers of the Poor of the said Parish of Bicknoller to convey the said James Jennings and Harriet his wife and Martha John Mary and James their said children from, and out of the Parish of Bicknoller aforesaid, to the said Parish of Stogumber and them to deliver to the Churchwardens and Overseers of the Poor there, or to some or one of them, together with this our Order, or a true Copy thereof, at the same time showing to them the Original. And We do also hereby require you the said Churchwardens and Overseers of the Poor of the said Parish of Stogumber to receive and provide for them as Inhabitants of your Parish'.*

About the same time, the churchwardens and overseers of the poor in Bicknoller informed their counterparts in Stogumber that unless an appeal was lodged against the decision, James and family would be dispatched to their parish. Stogumber had to appeal within the statutory time limit, which was before the next meeting of the Quarter Sessions. As the hearing took place in August, the appeal

---

6. He was actually 43.

7. If these dates were accurate only his mother was still alive as his father died in 1811.

8. But only just!

9. That would have been about 1814/15, but he was buried in Stogumber on 30th June 1811.

10. In fact, she had died five years earlier as she was buried in Stogumber on 27th April 1834.

would have to be received by October, the time of the next Quarter Sessions. All the papers relating to the case, including the examinations of James and John, were forwarded to the relevant parties in Stogumber.

If the removal order was carried out, the family, along with their meagre possessions loaded onto a handcart, would have been escorted by the constable for Bicknoller to the boundary between the two parishes. From there the officials in Stogumber would take over and find some accommodation for them. As stated earlier, the nature of poor relief had changed from 'outdoor' to 'indoor' under the terms of the Poor Law Amendment Act of 1834. In many cases, it led to automatic entry into the workhouse. There were some exceptions and, as there were four dependent children involved, the family might have been treated more sympathetically. According to 'The Victoria County History', there was a workhouse in use in Stogumber until 1840 but the parish also owned cottages to house three families, so is that where they went?

No record of the outcome has been found, so it's impossible to state with certainty what actually happened. However, it is known that sometimes an order was not acted upon immediately and a family could stay in the parish which was trying to oust them. The two parishes in dispute could have come to an agreement to leave the family where they were living, i.e. in Bicknoller, with the chargeable parish, Stogumber, agreeing to maintain them. The issue was further clouded by a complaint, dated 15th November 1839, made to one of the Justices of the Peace, TC Luxton, by an overseer of the poor in Stogumber. John Tuckfield, a farmer, made the following statement: *'To my knowledge James Jennings late of the parish of Stogumber aforesaid Carpenter has deserted his wife and family for one month and upwards whereby she and they have become chargeable to the said parish of Stogumber. The said James Jennings is able to maintain himself and family by work but he has wilfully neglected to do. I therefore pray justice in the premises'.* [11]

What was going on here? James, it seems, had returned, forcibly, to attend the hearing only to disappear again. Does *'one month and upwards'* mean he had hung around for a while and then skedaddled when the dust had settled a little? Why had the overseer not registered his complaint until three months after the hearing took place? At this point I began to question whether we had actually heard the last of James because the authorities were still clearly anxious to catch up with him. It seems unlikely they would have gone to the time, trouble and expense simply to decide his place of legal settlement without

exacting justice for Harriet. There was every reason to continue their pursuit as long as his family continued to rely on poor relief. The fact that close to one third of the population in Stogumber in 1834 was supported by the parish was justification enough to want to avoid burdening the ratepayers unnecessarily.

I contacted Somerset Record Office to see if there were records showing further payments to the family in either parish, but there were not. Fortunately, in the overseers' accounts for Bicknoller and Stogumber, there were references to subsequent attempts to find James. Just before the complaint made by Stogumber's overseer on 15th November 1839 about the injustice of the parish having to maintain his family, there was an entry in Bicknoller's overseers' accounts [12] as follows:

1839
November 11   Paid to Mr George Blake a bill for fetching James Jennings £1 0s 0d

I suspect that this referred to the occasion on 1st August when he was apprehended, the payment to the constable being somewhat delayed. Since Bicknoller was no longer responsible for the family, there would have been no obligation to continue the search on behalf of the parish's ratepayers.

A couple of years went by before James's name cropped up again, this time in Stogumber's overseers' accounts 1836-1845. [13] The page, headed *'Disbursted'* [14] shows the following entry on 21st February 1842:

Overseers Expenses to Apprehend James Jenning (sic) *£1 19s 3d*

Just over a year later, on 27th April 1843, there he was again, under the heading *'Payment, Quarter ending Mitsumer* (sic)*1843'*:

Expenses of A Journey to Taunton & Wellington in Search of James Jenning (sic) *who has deserted his Wife & Family 10s 0d*

The taxpayers had a better deal this time at ten bob [15] but it looks like another false trail. Finally, it seems that one last attempt was undertaken to trace him for, on 22nd March 1845, this was recorded in Stogumber's accounts:

Expenses incurred in endeavouring to Apprehend James Jenning (sic) *who had left his Wife and Family. £1 15s 0d*

11. The word 'premises' here is a legal term, meaning matters referred to previously.
12. Ref: D/P/bic 13/2/36.
13. Ref: D/P/stogm 13/2/6.
14. Somerset for 'Disbursed'.
15. Slang for ten shillings.

Was the increased cost due to inflation or did it reflect the time spent and distance covered as he had been spotted further away? The two parishes had paid out a total of £5 4s 3d to track him down but all to no avail. I'm beginning to feel sorry, not only for the parishioners of Bicknoller and Stogumber, whose money had been wasted (not just a modern phenomenon then), but also for James who really was a hunted man. Part of me hopes the poor bugger did get away, but I also feel that he should have been forced to pay maintenance for his wife and kids.

The irregular intervals between the searches suggest that sightings of James had been reported to the officials in Stogumber, who felt obliged to follow them up. It's not clear why he was pursued for nearly six years for, as I said, there were no records found of payments made to the family during that period, unless it was to force him to provide for them. Indeed, we know that Harriet was working, first as an agricultural labourer and then as a washerwoman, so she was supporting her children. A runaway husband, if caught, could be prosecuted, but it doesn't look as though this happened to James. Anyway, in the end, I suppose it made more sense financially to let him go – if he had been detained and imprisoned he still wouldn't have been taking care of his family.

Meanwhile, what was he up to while the authorities conducted periodic searches for him? One thing is certain, he must have been aware that they wouldn't give up easily, which meant he'd have to keep on the move and put as much distance between him and them as possible. Wembdon had proved too close for comfort so when I next located him he was in Meare, not far from Glastonbury. Not only had he just about doubled the distance from his pursuers this time, but he appeared on the 1841 census of Meare as - surprise, surprise - none other than James Appledore. It could be argued that this was perfectly legitimate as that was his name in the baptismal register. Why would he have done that, if not to fool those looking for him? He was hoping that enough time had elapsed for hardly anyone to recall the family's alias, which had largely died out by the beginning of the nineteenth century, always supposing anyone other than the enumerator could read it. According to the census, he was said to be aged 40 and a journeyman carpenter. His actual age was 44, but once again it was consistent with the rounding-down procedure of the time. Unfortunately, there was no indication of the place where he was staying, but the two men recorded above and below his name were described as 'inmates'. The word 'inmate' seems to have been crossed through in both instances, and the absence of the mark on this form to denote each new household makes it impossible to tell exactly where he was staying.

For the next ten years nothing is known of his whereabouts, and it wasn't until the following census of 1851 that he surfaced again. He had left Somerset and headed off to Chagford in Devon, where he was working as a servant and living in Fore Street. Apart from his age, which was shown as 46 when he would have been about 54, everything else seems to point to it being him. His occupation was listed as 'millwright journeyman', his place of birth as 'Stogumber, Somerset' and he was described as 'married'. The other occupants of the household were interesting: three unmarried sisters (whose brother was head of the family but absent on the day) aged 27, 23 and 17. There was one other servant, a widower, also a journeyman millwright. If this James Jennings was Harriet's missing husband, what would she have made of this set-up, had she known? But that, regrettably, is where James' story ended. He escaped the clutches of the Stogumber Stasi but there was no avoiding the long arm of the Grim Reaper. How, when and where he died remains a mystery as I have been unable to find a death certificate for him. There surely must be one, if he remained in this country, and I can only hope that one day it will come to light.

When I embarked upon the ancestral trail, I vowed that I would not be judgmental about the conduct of my forebears as I couldn't possibly empathise with their situation close to two centuries later. Nevertheless, it is difficult to avoid the conclusion that my great-great-grandfather was a ne'er-do-well and I am descended from the black sheep of the family. Why did he behave so badly, and could there be any extenuating circumstances? With very little to go on, the known facts seem overwhelmingly damning of his conduct, but maybe there are some indications to the contrary to be found. As the youngest of Thomas and Sarah's nine children, I expect he was well and truly surplus to requirements. Twenty-two years younger than his eldest brother, John (more of whom later), he might have been overshadowed by some of his siblings and, blessed with rather less initiative, did not become independent as fast as his peers. We know, for example, from his own testimony at the settlement hearing, that he was living either with his parents or one of his brothers until well into adulthood. After he left the relative security of working and boarding with his brother John, he could have continued to live with his mother. When the lease on the property she had shared with her husband expired, it sounds from John's testimony as though she had left there, so could she and James have set up home elsewhere in Stogumber? Is it coincidence that John was ordered to support his mother from about 1832, the same year that James married Harriet? My point is that he might not have had to fend for himself, and to be saddled suddenly with a wife and child must have come as something of a shock.

I question why he hadn't taken up a formal apprenticeship, but instead worked for his brothers without any written agreement. The time he spent working for them amounted to that of an apprenticeship, i.e. seven years. Lack of funding was no bar as the parish used to pay for those in reduced circumstances. Without an indenture, he deprived himself of the chance to become a master craftsman but instead remained a journeyman carpenter/millwright – an unqualified workman who hired out his labour to an employer on a daily basis. An apprenticeship also afforded the opportunity to obtain a legal settlement in the parish where you were apprenticed. James admitted that he had never taken steps to gain a legal settlement anywhere, but he must have been aware of how vitally important it was to be legally settled in case you fell on hard times, a very real prospect for the labouring classes. So, an opportunity to obtain a relatively more secure future was missed. What a pillock!

James married quite late – he was about 36 – even for that era, when most people did so during their 20s. Once he and Harriet had a family, it became even more imperative to have a legal settlement, as, without it, their welfare was jeopardised if their father could not, or would not, provide for them. Clearly, being an older parent did not make him a more responsible one. As a result of his inertia, the family was reduced to the level of paupers and, as we have seen, became the subject of an unseemly squabble between two parishes, neither of which was willing to maintain them. Why was he so neglectful of his duties as a husband and father: firstly, to work and provide for his family and, secondly, never to have taken measures to ensure their wellbeing if he became incapable of supporting them? Perhaps the burden of family life was too great for him and he buckled under the strain. Did he have some kind of mental breakdown, and the temptation to escape it all and regain his freedom became too difficult to resist? Whatever the truth of the matter – and we'll never know – James seems to have been a weak, inadequate specimen at best, and feckless, selfish and idle at worst. His actions, viewed from any generation, cannot be classed as decent or honourable. Was he a free spirit or a useless git? My money's on the latter.

Whilst James was leading an apparently itinerant life, what of Harriet and his children? As an abandoned wife, she must have found herself in dire circumstances. Even though desertion was quite a common occurrence in those days (yet another parallel with modern times), it was no doubt a source of great shame in itself (unlike today), and women often referred to themselves as widows. In order to feed and clothe her children, she had been forced into seeking poor relief, which was very reluctantly granted, understandably, as her husband was deemed capable of working. I like to think of her as an independent, feisty woman who'd had enough of the shabby treatment meted out to her by men and, having no desire to be a charity case, found herself a job. From the record of the children's baptisms in 1840, we know that she and the four children were living in Yard. The events of 1839 might have influenced her decision to have Martha

baptised a second time. Although baptism itself afforded no right to a legal settlement, it might have helped Martha's case should she have wished to gain one in Bicknoller at a later date.

The census of Bicknoller in 1841 reveals that they were still in Yard and Harriet had found work as an agricultural labourer. She might have had help in this from James Pocock, who was a farmer, and later employed Martha as a house servant at Navis Farm in Stogumber (1851 census). He and his wife eventually became Harriet's neighbours, as the 1861 census of Bicknoller shows Harriet and son John living in Cottage No 1, with James and Elizabeth Pocock in Cottage No 2 in Yard. Pocock was then aged 74, retired and described as a *'Chelsea Pensioner'*.

At least the family had a roof over its head but it must have been a huge struggle for Harriet to look after her children whilst working as an agricultural labourer. Sometime between 1841 and 1851 she changed her job and became a washerwoman, which was also extremely strenuous work. You only have to look at the equipment used by the Victorians to do their laundry to realise that it was, physically, a very demanding task. How much of such apparatus was available to her we cannot know, but she was living near the Doniford stream which would have been the likely source of water. I suppose she took in washing for the better-off farmers' wives and the like.

Gradually, three of the children left home and John was the only one living with his mother by the time of the 1861 census. Then aged 24, he was working as a railway labourer. I have been unable to trace Mary's whereabouts but she left home between the 1851 and 1861 censuses, as did James, the youngest, who was my great-grandfather. The 1861 census was the final one on which Harriet appeared, but there was one possible mention of her on 1st February 1866 in 'A Bicknoller Diary 1860-1868' which was compiled by Paul Mansfield, using records such as the churchwardens' accounts. In a list of the houses and

Occupier	Owner	Description	Name of Property
Pocock & Jennings	Mrs Pocock	house & gdn	Yard

occupants, drawn up in order to set the rates, we find:
If this does refer to Harriet, she would have been about 59 years old, so in the five years before the next census of 1871 she had either left Bicknoller or died. A very unsatisfactory note to end on as I would like to know what finally happened to the woman who was my great-great-grandmother. Her life was certainly very hard. I hope that at least one of her children was able to care for her in her old age and that she didn't die in the workhouse. In an age when death certificates were issued, it is strange that

there is, as yet, no trace of one for James or Harriet. I intend to continue the search in order to close that particular chapter of the family's history.

Before moving on to the next generation, to try to rescue the reputation of the Jennings ancestry, I looked at the lives of James's two brothers in a little more detail. Thomas and John must have worked with him closely to equip him with a trade, so they were in for a disappointment at the way he turned out. Their lives, in stark contrast to his, seem exemplary in comparison. I begin with John, the eldest of Thomas and Sarah's children, who was baptised on 20th February 1774. He married Martha Duddridge on 3rd July 1812 at Crowcombe, when he was 38 years old and she was a little older, in her early 40s. There was no record of them having any children. From the settlement hearing in 1839, it is known that John was a millwright. He must have been quite a skilled craftsman, able to work with both metal and wood, and involved in the building and maintenance of wind- and water-mills and the related machinery. This meant that he would have been well qualified to instruct his young brother in *joining and millwrighting'*. As almost every manor house had its mill, where tenants would pay to grind their corn, there was no shortage of work so John was able to earn a good living from his trade.

James was working for John in Stogumber for about four years from around 1816 to 1820, so it was sometime later that John and Martha had made the move to Bicknoller, where it seems that he was sufficiently well-off to lease property and sub-let some of it. I discovered this information from the Bicknoller Apportionment Map which was compiled in 1838. This is a vast document, beautifully hand-written, containing details of all the land and properties in the village at that time. It shows the landowners, occupiers and the name and description of land and premises, along with the acreage and the rents payable. The Tithe Commutation Act of 1836 converted a tax in kind under the old tithe system (in which a tenth of all agricultural produce, including livestock, was given up to support the parish priest) to an annual rent on land. Tithe commissioners were appointed to oversee this change, which resulted in the production of a map for every parish in the country, showing how it was divided up into parcels of land. Each plot was allocated a number on the map which corresponded with the details outlined in the accompanying section of the document. Numbers 193 and 194 on the Bicknoller map refer to land and premises at Culverhayes. Beneath the heading *'Landowners'* was written *'John Jennings Lessee under the Dean and Chapter of Wells'*. At last, an ancestor with some initiative and enterprise! Number 193 consisted of a *'House containing 3 Dwellings and a Garden',* and 194

was an orchard. The total area amounted to just over an acre and the rent charged was 11 shillings. The occupiers were *'Thomas Jennings and others'*. The overseers' accounts for Bicknoller in 1832 confirm that the house was divided into three, with each family paying one third of the rent for it and the orchard. Although Thomas was living there in 1832, John was not one of the other two tenants at this time, so he and Martha must have moved there sometime between then and 1838. In 1838, then, the three brothers were living in close proximity, with James in Yard and John and Thomas in Culverhayes. This was a situation that was not destined to last with the disappearance of James in 1839.

During his examination at James's settlement hearing, John revealed that he had been supporting his mother, Sarah, during the last years of her life, at the behest of the parish officials in Stogumber. This is a clear indication that John was a man of some means, possibly the only family member who was in a position to maintain her. (It wouldn't have been much use relying on James if his conduct after her death was anything to go by.) It has to be said that John was ordered to do so – the parish had the power to demand maintenance from a well-off close relative for those without the means to provide for themselves. Apparently, Sarah wasn't living with John and Martha as her abode in the burial register was recorded as Williton, although she was buried in Stogumber on 27th April 1834. She had reached the grand old age of 83 (she was baptised on 20th April 1751), something of an achievement when the contemporary average life expectancy was under 50.

John's wife, Martha, was not quite so fortunate. Shortly after the 1841 census was taken, she died, aged about 71, and on 29th June she was buried in Stogumber. Just over a year later, John too was dead, at the age of 68. I found this out from a copy of his will, which was handed to me on one of my visits to the record office. Dated 15th October 1841, it was one of the most poignant documents I came across in the course of my research. Judging by the date, it looks as though it had been made in response to the death of his wife and almost certainly confirms that they had no children. This copy of the original will, which would have been entered into a ledger by a clerk for the ecclesiastical probate court, contained some rather creative spelling which makes me wonder if it was written by a lawyer or by John himself. Here it is reproduced in its entirety, apart from the signatures at the end, as to quote from it wouldn't convey the quirkiness of it:

'This is the last Will and Testament of me John Jennings of the parish of Bicknoller in the County of Somerset Millwright made despossion [16] of all such Wordly goods and effects which hath pleased the Almighty God to bless

16. Presumably this means 'dispossession' or 'disposal'.

me with in this life. I give the same as flows [17] *First I give the sum of Seventy pounds, that is, Sixty pounds in the Saving Bank at Taunton ten pounds to be added on to it from my effects with intres* [18] *as from the Saving Bank. I give the same to John Mills/Abraham George Mills/Wm Henery* (sic) *Mills three sons of my sister Elizabeth Mills and Wm Mills now living near the Hot Wells Bristol. Also I give to Henry Chidgey my Brother in Law the sum of Eight pound to be paid the month after my deces* [19] *Also I apoint Isaac Jennings son of my Brother Thomas Jennings hole and sole Executor of this my last Will and Testament. Whereof I the said John Jennings the Testator have set my Hand and Seal this fiften day of October One Thousand Eight hundred forty one'.* [20]

Having found nothing but abject poverty in the records relating to the family, it was quite a surprise to be presented with a will; even more so to find it contained reference to a savings account which, along with the rest of John's estate, amounted to about 70 pounds, a not inconsiderable sum for the time. It does seem that John had worked hard to save it, so how sad that neither he nor Martha lived to enjoy the fruits of his labour. Without children of his own, his nephews and brother-in-law became the beneficiaries. His sister's sons must have been special as he had many nieces and nephews to chose from, so perhaps he was godfather to one or all three of them. It is impossible to tell why Henry Chidgey benefited in preference to any of John's siblings. Henry had married John's sister Martha in 1819 and was a witness at the marriage of James and Harriet in 1832. The executor, Isaac Jennings, had the task of carrying out John's instructions but received nothing according to the terms of the will.

It was witnessed by Simon Wine and John Saunders. Curious to know who these two were, I searched the Bicknoller census for 1841 and found them both. Simon Wine, aged 25, was a machine maker and mender, living in Chilcombe. John Saunders, who was 30, was a blacksmith and lived at South Lynch. Both would have featured prominently in the community, as they provided services essential to the life of the village. Saunders, for example, mended the school's gate in 1866, and Wine was asked to fix a threshing machine which had gone beyond repair. The owner insisted that he wanted it mended and then refused to pay. The case went to court and was settled in Wine's favour. (Incidents described in 'A Bicknoller Diary 1860-1868'.)

The circumstances surrounding John's death came as a shock as it wasn't from natural causes - he was killed by a

fall from a stepladder. The accident happened on 22nd October 1842 at Coombe Lowersmiths in the parish of Kilve so it looks as though he was working away from home. There were various mills in the area so maybe he was still engaged as a millwright at the age of 68. The coroner at Langport was informed but I have not been able to find a copy of his report into the accident. The death was registered on 25th October and the cause on the certificate was recorded as *'Accident by a fall from a Step Ladder'*. His relatives, in particular his brother, Thomas, I would imagine, must have been notified and arranged for the body to be returned to Stogumber, where he was buried on 27th October, just five days after the accident. Although Kilve isn't very far from Stogumber and the journey home was probably made by horse and cart, that was a pretty quick turn around for an unexpected death. And so the life of John Jennings had ended in tragic circumstances.

Now, a look at Thomas Jennings, who was the third child born to Thomas and Sarah. He was baptised in Stogumber on 30th November 1777 so he was almost four years younger than John and more than 18 years older than James. Thomas married Rebekah Davis, by banns, in Tolland on 11th May 1805 when he was nearly 28 and she was about 21. Neither signed their names but each made a mark in the register with possibly the thickest quill pen of all time. Despite that, one of their witnesses was able to write his signature very clearly and that was brother John. Their entry in the register looks like a page from a schoolboy's notebook on his first attempt at using pen and ink – all blots and smudges.

Between 1806 and 1828, Thomas and Rebekah produced 11 children. The first four were baptised in Stogumber between 1806 and 1812, whilst the remaining seven were baptised in Bicknoller between 1815 and 1828. At his settlement hearing, James had stated that he had worked for Thomas in Bicknoller from about 1812 or 1813, remaining with him for about three years. This confirms that Thomas and Rebekah had been living in Stogumber until around 1812 and then moved to Culverhayes in Bicknoller. Culverhayes was given as their abode when their fifth child, Mary, was baptised on 26th November 1815.

After the birth of their seventh child in 1819, the family was in financial difficulty, forcing Thomas to ask for poor relief on 7th July 1819. [21] Fortunately, in 1795 the Speenhamland Act had been passed, enabling the working poor to receive assistance if their wages weren't sufficient to support the family. (Unluckily for some, a later Act in

17. Follows.
18. Interest.
19. Decease.
20. Ref: DD/ED/187/905.
21. Ref: D/P/bic 13/3/73.

1834 changed the system to entry into the workhouse to discourage the idle, not always successfully.) Even so, relief was not readily given by the overseer in Bicknoller, William Addams, and the case was referred to two of His Majesty's Justices of the Peace in Nettlecombe, as there was no select vestry (parish council) in Bicknoller at this time. Addams was present at the hearing but failed to give any reason why relief should not be granted. The Justices, Henry Tripp and Rev John Matthew, were impressed by Thomas, saying that, as his wages were not enough to keep his family *'we the said justices having taken into consideration the character and conduct of the said Thomas Jennings do for the special cause herein before stated do* (sic) *hereby order the Churchwardens and Overseers of the Poor of the said parish of Bicknoller ... to pay unto the said Thomas Jennings the Sum of Three Shillings and sixpence weekly, and every Week, for and towards his Support and Maintenance, for one month from the date hereof or until such Time as they shall be otherwise ordered according to Law to forbear the said Allowance'*. So, Thomas Jennings one, William Addams nil.

The following month, on 4th August, Thomas was back and, once again, Addams opposed payment, but still could not produce a good reason to refuse it [22]. The same two Justices in Nettlecombe overruled Addams's decision, this time stating that they *'do find as the special cause of granting the Relief hereby directed to be made that His said family are too numerous and of too young an age to maintain or provide for themselves'*. To add insult to injury, as far as Addams was concerned, they ordered that payment should be increased to four shillings weekly with the same conditions as before. The situation could not have been made any easier for the family with the birth of four more children between 1821 and 1828. You do wonder how parents of that era, struggling to cope with such a large family, would have reacted to each addition to the family. Would it have been a case of 'Aren't we fortunate to have so many of our children survive?' or 'Oh gawd, another mouth to feed'. The family's poverty might have been the reason James left Thomas's employment after three years. Not only did he have to keep his young brother during the week but he was also paying him two shillings weekly, which must have been an added strain on their meagre resources.

Their abode in Bicknoller could not have been very large, as we have seen from the overseers' accounts for 1832 that Thomas was renting one third of a house and one third of an orchard at Culverhayes. He was paying five pence for the house and one penny and three farthings for the orchard. His neighbours, George Symes and Robert Carrott were charged the same for their share. Later on, as already mentioned, John became his landlord, as well as his neighbour, when he leased the premises from the Dean and Chapter of Wells.

The records also show that Thomas, who was a carpenter, was paid by the parish for making coffins. One occasion, probably in about 1832, speaks graphically of the hardship endured by the poor, for it referred to the burial of a pauper child. As well as the ten shillings and nine pence paid to Thomas, the parish paid for two yards of calico for a shroud and five shillings for a grave. It must have been heartbreaking being unable to afford to bury your own child.

Another reference to Thomas is interesting as it featured in the accounts of William Addams, the overseer who had refused him poor relief, but this time he was paying him 18 shillings for a coffin for William Lackham. These accounts, [23] dated 18th March 1833 to 17th March 1834, show that John Hensley received four shillings for preparing the grave, and James Grandfield three shillings and sixpence for a shroud. (It's a true saying that one person's loss is someone else's gain.) Then, something rather drastic must have befallen gravedigger Hensley because Thomas was paid 18 shillings for a coffin for him, and John Marquis ten shillings *'for going for the Coroner for the late John Hensley'*. It looks like a sudden and unexpected demise rather than from natural causes, as there would have been no need to inform the coroner. I looked at the 1841 census, which took place several years after his death where I found Anne Hensley, still living in Bicknoller, aged 50 and working as an agricultural labourer. Was this John's widow? It seems very likely as living with her was her son John, also an agricultural labourer at the age of 15, her daughter Elizabeth, aged 12, and another son, James, who was eight. Assuming husband and wife were of similar age, John died before his time, leaving another young family fatherless. 'Larkrise to Candleford' it was not [24].

Thomas himself died in 1846, four years after his brother John, and he was buried in Bicknoller Churchyard, along with his wife Rebekah, who outlived him by 13 years or so. The inscription on the headstone reads:

'Sacred to the memory of Thomas Jennings of this parish who departed this life on Nov 22 1846. Aged 69 years'
'Also Rebekah wife of the above, who departed this life April 28 1860. Aged 76 years'

John and Thomas had probably spent their entire lives in Stogumber and Bicknoller, and seem to have been decent,

---

22. Ref: D/P/bic 13/3/69.
23. Ref: D/P/bic 13/2/25.
24. With reference to the BBC's sentimental portrayal of Flora Thompson's book of that title.

hardworking men. I suppose there's always a chance they might have been a couple of wife-beating drunks but there is no evidence to suggest that. There are clues to the contrary in the statements taken when Thomas and then James sought poor relief. John had maintained his mother for several years and worked hard to have a tidy sum stashed away in the bank. Thomas had impressed the Justices of the Peace, as he was willing to work but couldn't earn enough to provide for his ever-expanding family. Both had shouldered the responsibility for teaching their brother a trade, and his conduct was no reflection on them. If James had been aware of their deaths, he could not have returned to pay his respects, as he would have been nabbed by the constable.

The tales of my ancestors reflect the lives of many others living at that time and give us an inkling of what life was like in the nineteenth-century English village. Poor though they undoubtedly were, it seems to me that the inhabitants were much better off than those in the towns and cities. That is not to suggest that Bicknoller and Stogumber were the quiet, rural idyll they are today. There were many quarries in the vicinity, some no longer in use but others still being worked. At times, the area must have been rocked by the sound of blasting, which increased when the building of the railway was under way. The records show that drunkenness was widespread – there was a brewery in Stogumber – with no shortage of drinking houses, licensed or illicit. This led to frequent disputes and outbreaks of brawling (once again, not much has changed). The coming of the railway significantly altered the character of the landscape, and had a huge impact on the life of the population, bringing about changes as dramatic as air travel has in our own era. For a start, it became easier to move out of your native parish and find work elsewhere in order to improve your standard of living, which is exactly what my great-grandfather, James, eventually decided to do.

STOGUMBER: The Church of St Mary the Virgin, 1979.

PART 2 - A FAMILY HISTORY:
JAMES and SARAH JENNINGS

As we have seen, the young James's life did not get off to an auspicious start – he was abandoned by his father when he was just a few weeks old and then immortalised as *'Jane'* in the Baptismal Register. And this certainly turned out to be prophetic.

The father's conduct must have had quite a profound effect on his kids' childhood which, in those days, was an all-too-brief experience anyway. In fact, the distinction between childhood and adulthood was so blurred it seems as though it hardly existed. For generations, childhood had been synonymous with the world of work, when the country's economy was based on agriculture. But when that began to change during the Industrial Revolution, there took place a shameful and shocking episode in the nation's history. Children as young as five or six, mainly orphans or drawn from the pauper class, were put to work in the mills and mines. In conditions akin to slavery, their labour was used to press ahead with industrialisation so that Britain could maintain its lead over its rivals. Gradually, as the nineteenth century wore on, it became apparent that the iniquitous treatment of the young could not be tolerated in a supposedly Christian country. It took a long time for reform to take place. Unsurprisingly, Parliament was slow to act as the interests of manufacturers and mine owners were diametrically opposed to those of the exploited children, who were being callously robbed of their childhood. Several Acts were passed to regulate and limit the number of hours they could work, but it wasn't until near the end of the century that real improvement came about with the availability of education to all. Although the very young had worked during the country's agrarian past, it was those slaving away in the mines and factories whose plight had inspired long-overdue change. It's a sobering thought that we owe a debt of gratitude to the generations of children who were so cruelly deprived of their childhood before it was fully recognised as a time to be protected and cherished.

It's unlikely that James and his siblings suffered such a fate, but from an early age they would have been expected to earn a few coppers to contribute to the upkeep of the family. It's hard to believe that their mother could have coped on her income alone. There is no evidence that any of them received any formal education and they probably remained illiterate throughout their lives. This was not uncommon, as demonstrated by the census of Bicknoller in 1841, when no children were recorded as scholars.

Opposite - BICKNOLLER: St George's Church, 1979.

Although the situation had improved by the time of the next census, when there were 23 scholars, many still did not attend school. The contemporary educational provision in Bicknoller was described as 'deplorable' (The Victoria County History, A History of Somerset Vol V) so it sounds as though the Jennings offspring didn't miss much. Without an apprenticeship, James and his brother, John, were unskilled, their most likely employment being agricultural labouring, while their sister, Martha, worked as a *'house servant'* for Farmer James Pocock. The proposal, then, to build the West Somerset Railway on their doorstep must have seemed like a massive stroke of good fortune to the likes of James and John.

The first public indication that a line was to be constructed in order to connect the West Somerset area to the Bristol & Exeter Railway (which amalgamated with the Great Western Railway on 1st January 1876) came in the announcement that a meeting would take place in Williton at the Egremont Hotel on 9th July 1856. James was then 17 years old, and the prospect of a better living could not have been lost on him and his contemporaries. It was almost three years later, on 7th April 1859, that the ceremony to 'cut the first sod' occurred near what was to be Crowcombe Heathfield Station. According to Ian Coleby (in 'The Minehead Branch'), 60 navvies were present, waiting to start work. Could James and John Jennings have been among them? There is a very strong possibility that they were for, as Coleby (ibid) says, the navvies who built this line were not drafted in, as was the case with other railways. They all lived locally with their families or as lodgers. He conducted a survey of the 1861 census of the surrounding area and found that 'around 150 men, describing themselves as railway labourers, were resident'. There was also an absence of the customary camps set up for navvies when a line was under construction. It is almost certain then that James started work on the West Somerset Railway from its inception, when he was 20 years old. If he wasn't fit and strong already, he surely was soon after for the job was, physically, exceptionally hard, carried out with picks, shovels and wheelbarrows, aided by horses and wagons. Although arduous, it was a better proposition than agricultural labouring, and not just financially. It offered more security of tenure for, even after the construction work was finished, labourers would be required for the maintenance of the track.

There wasn't much opportunity for advancement at James's level, but his prospects were such that he was able to marry at a much younger age than his father had, though true to form, it was a 'shotgun' affair. His marriage to Sarah Hurley took place in the parish church of Stogumber on 23rd November 1860. The ceremony was conducted by the curate, E. Otto Trevelyan, in the presence of the two witnesses, John Jennings, brother of James, and Jane Coles, who was Sarah's elder sister. James's age was correctly recorded as 21, but Sarah, also said to be 21, was in fact 19. She could have been uncertain of her precise age and made an innocent mistake. On the other hand, as minors required parental permission to marry, was this a deliberate deception? Were her parents opposed to her marriage to James? As Sarah was in the very advanced stages of pregnancy – their son John was born just a few weeks later – it seems unlikely as illegitimacy was regarded as scandalous. During this era, many unmarried mothers were cast out by their families because of the disgrace. Herber (in 'Ancestral Trails') says that many brides still went to the altar pregnant, despite the shame and the disapproval of the church.

What on earth the curate must have thought as he joined James and Sarah, a very obvious pair of 'sinners', in holy matrimony can only be imagined. Maybe the voluminous skirts of the period largely concealed that Sarah was 'up the duff'. He had officiated in place of the vicar, who was his brother, George Trevelyan, as the latter suffered from mental illness. (Possibly the sight of so many pregnant brides had brought home to him the utter futility of his preaching and had driven him nuts.) Despite this, George was the incumbent from 1820 to 1871, whilst E. Otto, clearly made of sterner stuff, was the resident curate until 1869.

So what is known of the young woman James Jennings married? Using material gathered from official records such as census returns and registration certificates, I was able to gain a little insight into her family life. Sarah Hurley came into the world on 27th February 1841 at Combe Cross Lane in Stogumber, the youngest of the seven children born to James and Mary Hurley. She had four brothers and two sisters, and their father was an agricultural labourer at the time of her birth. Also living in Combe Cross Lane were Mary Hurley's parents, Charles and Ann Routley, and their unmarried daughter, Elizabeth.

Shortly after Sarah was born, the 1841 census took place on 6th June, and her age was recorded correctly as four months (one of the few occasions in her life when it was right). Omitted from this census was her brother, Robert, who would have been four or five years old, but he could have been staying with relatives. Ten years later, in 1851, it seems that the family, still living in Stogumber, had fallen on hard times as James Hurley was said to be an

agricultural labourer and pauper. He might have been in receipt of poor relief to augment the extremely low wages paid to agricultural workers. It is difficult to assess why this situation had occurred since, of the five children still living at home, four were in employment: Jane, aged 21 was a charwoman, Harriet a seamstress, and Robert and William were agricultural labourers. Sarah was described as a scholar, which, if true, doesn't say much for the quality of education in Stogumber either. As she marked official documents with an X, it looks as though she too remained illiterate throughout her life. (Perhaps children were recorded as scholars if they were of school age, regardless of whether they attended school or not.) The eldest son, Charles, an agricultural labourer, had married and was lodging at the home of William Burge, a Greenwich pensioner, and his wife, Susan. Charles and his wife, Mary, had a one-year-old child, Elizabeth Ann.

By the time of the next census on 7th April 1861, James and Sarah Jennings and their four-month-old son, John, were sharing a dwelling with Sarah's brother, Robert, his wife Harriet and their two-month-old son, Arthur James, at Old Way in Stogumber. James and Robert were both recorded as railway labourers. Still living in Stogumber with his wife (all the children had left home) was Sarah's father, James Hurley, who had found work as a 'brewer's labourer', no doubt at the nearby Stogumber Brewery, which was founded by Charles George Elers in 1840. The eldest brother, Charles, had also become a railway labourer and father to five children, Elizabeth Ann, now aged 11, John (eight), William (five), Mary Jane (two) and Anna Maria (eight months). I mention them because this was the first time I had encountered children being given two Christian names – why only the girls? How much easier it would have been to trace ancestors more clearly identifiable with the addition of a middle name, especially the males. Young John also caught my attention as he was said to be working as a 'Plough Boy'. Some 60 years later, so was my father, but not at the tender age of eight. I was also interested to note that Charles now had a boarder, one William Brown, aged 44 and unmarried, who had been born in Kings Lynn, Norfolk, a long way from Somerset. It was no surprise to see that Brown was a railway labourer, one incidence of how people were beginning to travel to where they could find work as the railway network started to open up the whole country. Ten years earlier, villages were mainly populated by those who had been born in the county. The 1851 census of Bicknoller showed that almost all the residents were born there or in the neighbouring parishes, with just a few hailing from elsewhere, principally Devon and Dorset. The same pattern was probably repeated in villages all over the country, and it's difficult to overestimate the profound changes brought about by the railway system. As we shall see, James Jennings availed himself of the opportunity to move to another part of the country in search of work.

Before that happened, a couple of events took place which could have contributed to James's decision to leave Somerset. In 1867, Sarah's brother, Charles Hurley, was charged with stealing half a gallon of ale at Stogumber Station, along with Francis Reed, a railway policeman. The case was reported in the *West Somerset Free Press*, and, although many of the inhabitants would have been unable to read it, I'll bet the news spread through the village like wildfire. There was a great deal of petty, and more serious, crime (on this particular page of the newspaper there were five cases in the Stogumber area alone heard at Williton Petty Sessions on Thursday 4th July) but the charge against Hurley seems to have taken up rather more column inches than it merited. Thomas Redwood, an employee of the landlord of the inn close to Stogumber Station, was sent to collect a horse from a field near the station at about 6.15am on the day in question. There he claimed he saw Hurley draining ale out of a barrel, then replacing the peg in the cask once his half-gallon can was full. Redwood challenged Hurley and Reed with the words, *'Hallo: what be 'ee up to there?'* Hurley, apparently not amused, replied, *'What consarns thee? Thee'st better keep thy mouth shut, or else I'll kill thee'*. Somewhat of an overreaction perhaps, but it transpired that Redwood had a grudge against Reed, who had pushed him from the station platform some two months earlier. Redwood also admitted during cross-examination by the defendants' solicitor, a Mr Cook, that he told others he would not have split on Reed *'if Reed had not been always on with him'* – in other words there was a history of animosity between the two of them. A couple of witnesses were called, but after some legal wrangling the case was thrown out on the grounds that there wasn't enough evidence to secure a conviction. It certainly sounds as though Redwood viewed this as an opportunity to exact revenge on Reed, though why he would have wanted to implicate Hurley is unclear – unless of course there was some truth in Redwood's testimony. According to him, Hurley had visited him the next day at the innkeeper's stable to ask him to keep quiet about the incident, saying, *'I was only having a drop of returns what come back'*. What a palaver over half a gallon of beer. Redwood was fortunate not to have been prosecuted for wasting the court's time. I can just imagine the two 'villains' having a drop of ale to celebrate their acquittal, but I hope it wasn't nicked. Hurley's job was unaffected and he continued working as a railway labourer judging by the census of 1871. Incidentally, the ale was said to be the property of Charles Elers, the owner of the brewery where his father worked. Despite the prosecution being dropped, it must have been the subject of gossip, which would not be pleasant for the family in such a close-knit community. We're all familiar with the saying, 'There's no smoke without fire'.

It was followed by a happier occasion on 12th February 1868, when James and Sarah's second child was born.

(Almost an eight-year gap between the two sons suggests Sarah might have had miscarriages or stillborn babies during this time.) They named him James, and his birth was registered by his grandfather, James Hurley, on 20th March. Mystery surrounds this child, and, although there are good reasons to suppose that he didn't survive for very long, I've so far been unable to trace any record of his death. The date of his birth shows that his parents were still living in Stogumber during the early part of 1868, but, between then and the census of 1871, they left Somerset.

Viewed in the context of the time, when the mass movement of the population was still relatively in its infancy, it was a bold decision for James and Sarah to make. They were leaving behind their families for an uncertain future, and that must have caused them some apprehension. What prompted the move? I've mentioned the village gossip surrounding Charles Hurley's 'misdemeanour', the probable demise of their second son, James, and it could be that James's mother, Harriet, had died sometime in the 1860s. But, I suspect, overriding any unhappy memories was the fact that work on the West Somerset Railway had started to run out. Some workers would have been retained for track maintenance and the day-to-day running of the railway, but Sarah's brother, Robert, had become an agricultural labourer again by 1871. (The eldest, Charles, was still employed by the WSR – by the skin of his teeth.) It was not a prospect that appealed to James, who had somehow heard about the construction of a new line in Warwickshire. This was the East & West Junction Railway, which had been authorised by an Act of Parliament in 1864. Not the greatest choice, as it turned out to be somewhat unsuccessful and impoverished throughout its chequered history.

In the 1830s, after the building of the first public steam railway by George Stephenson, from Stockton to Darlington, there followed a period of 'Railway Mania', when railway companies were set up all over the country and the creation of many lines was underway. Although it required an Act of Parliament to authorise their construction, railways were not funded by the state but by private enterprise, with the result that some were better financed than others. There was no overall grand design but lines sprang up piecemeal and, at the height of the frenzy to get in on the act, some 250 companies were in operation. Eventually, the smaller ones would be swallowed up by the more prosperous, whilst others amalgamated or died out altogether until, by 1923, they were whittled down to four. A slump in the building of new lines duly followed in 1866 but picked up again to a lesser extent in the 1870s. With fewer lines under construction, James's options were limited and he had to go where there was work. Construction of the E&WJR had started in 1864 and the first section, a six-and-a-quarter mile single track from Fenny Compton to Kineton, opened on 1st June 1871; after another Act was passed in that year, the remainder of the line from Kineton to Stratford-upon-Avon was opened on 1st July 1873. Its purpose was to link the existing Northampton & Banbury Railway at Norton Green near Towcester with the Great Western Railway at Stratford.

It is not known exactly when James joined this Company, but the 1871 census shows that he was a railway labourer and would have been involved in the later stages of the building of this line. He was living with his wife at The Green in Northend, near Burton Dassett. He was said to be 31 (actually 32) and to have been born in *'Bignoler'* (sic) in the county of Somerset. (I guess the enumerator had some difficulty with the West Country accent.) There was no mention of their sons, John and James, but the census return for Stogumber shows that John, now a ten-year-old scholar, was staying with his grandparents, James and Mary Hurley, in Old Way. Little James might have accompanied his parents and died before the census, further evidence of his demise being the birth of a third son on 16th January 1873 at Northend who was also called James. As mentioned earlier, it wasn't unusual to name another child after a dead sibling – perhaps a strange practice to us, but done to ensure the continuation of a particular name down through the generations or in memory of the deceased.

On the baby's birth certificate, James is described as a *'Packer on Railway'*, suggesting that he was now in the permanent employment of the E&WJR. He was part of a gang of workers responsible for maintaining a specific length of track, usually one-and-a-half to two miles long. The ganger in charge walked the line daily to make sure that it was in good order and, if necessary, would direct his gang to tighten any nuts and bolts that had worked loose, knock in the oak keys and replenish ballast where required. I imagine the term 'packer' was derived from the latter task as it involved, according to Joby (in 'The Railwaymen'), 'packing ballast under sinking sleepers with the aid of jacks and shovels…'. Still bloody hard work then, but regarded as secure employment and, although the E&WJR didn't own any property, James would have been provided with rented accommodation, as at The Green.

The next 'momentous' occasion for the family was the arrival of my grandfather, Henry Charles Jennings, on 5th December 1876. By now, they had left Northend and were living in nearby Fenny Compton. James was still working for the E&WJR as a packer so the question is: why did he move? It seems as though the family had swapped a substantial stone or brick-built dwelling at The Green, in a pleasant village setting, for what was later described as a 'frame house' on the embankment near Fenny Compton Station. A 'frame house' is indicative of

a timber construction which was sited in a rather undesirable location. It must have been noisy, dirty and smoky, for not only did the E&WJR traffic pass through this station, but so did the express trains of the GWR, which also had a stopping place on the site. Of course, James would have had little say in where the company placed him, and I am indebted to John Jennings (SMJ archivist and no relation), who carried out extensive research on my behalf, for the most likely explanation for the move. He said that it was 'very convenient for an impoverished company such as the E&WJR to allow a platelayer to effectively be "on call" twenty-four hours a day. In the winter months the signalman would need to call out a "fog man" very often at short notice and the first choice for such a task was a local platelayer. Much time and therefore hold-ups could be saved if all the signalman had to do was walk up the yard to call out his man!' The move, then, was one of expediency and cost-cutting but maybe it included some kind of inducement, such as a promise of promotion. James did become a foreman platelayer, in charge of a gang of four or five men, but there is no indication of when this happened. There were a few perks too, like the plentiful supply of coal which had fallen from the wagons to heat your stove, and the opportunity to grow vegetables on the embankment, provided you were partial to a soot-covered variety. (I'm sure I've heard it said that soot does have horticultural benefits though I can't imagine what.)

By the time of my grandfather's birth, there were five members of the family living in the cottage near the station. John, the eldest son, had rejoined his parents at some stage, probably soon after they had settled in at The Green. According to the E&WJR's staff register,[1] he had started work for the company in 1876, when aged about 16. By 1881, he was married to a Fenny Compton girl, Elizabeth *('Betsey')* and had two children, Ann, aged two, and John, a month-old baby. A father at 19, John hadn't wasted much time in sampling the delights of the local talent. He was still working on the railway, living with his young family at 81 Brook Street. His mother, Sarah, had become a grandmother before giving birth to her fifth and final son, William, who was born on 16th April 1881.

Meanwhile, back in Stogumber, her father, James Hurley had died, aged 78, on 18th March 1880, from *'internal strangulation of the bowel'*, which was certified by J. Cocker, MRCS. Harriet Williams, one of Sarah's sisters, was said to have been present at the death and had informed the registrar. His widow, Mary, survived him by eight years and finally succumbed on 20th April 1888, aged 86. Her death certificate shows that she had been suffering from heart disease for four years and bronchitis for two days. A tough old bird. Her daughter, Harriet,

1. The National Archives, Ref: RAIL 674/11.

FENNY COMPTON: The School, 1978.

was present at her death too. Ten years or so had passed since Sarah's departure from Stogumber when her father died and about 18 years when her mother passed away. Did she see her parents at all during that time? The railway had certainly made it possible.

I wonder if the Hurleys met any of the younger grandsons, who all went to school in Fenny Compton in the 1880s. Fortunately, they benefited from the 1870 Elementary Education Act, which set up school boards throughout England and Wales to provide education for all children not already in school. Although it wasn't entirely free at this stage – that wasn't provided until 1891 – a school board was entitled to make attendance compulsory but fees for the very poor could be waived. Two further Acts in 1876 and 1880 prohibited the employment of children under ten and required them to attend school until the age of 13. James (born 16th January 1873) started school in 1880 when he was about seven. It seems as though his father or mother might have had a lapse of memory about his exact date of birth as it appears in the school's admissions register as '? April 1873' –

understandable if you weren't able to read or write. Charles (no mention of the name Henry now – he was in fact known as 'Charlie') entered school in 1881, aged five, and his younger brother William was about four when he started in 1885.

According to the next census in 1891 they were all at work. James, aged 18, was employed as an *'agricultural servant'* in Fenny Compton by Devon-born farmer, John Coombes, whilst Charles, aged 14 and the only son living with his parents near the station, was an agricultural labourer. William, who at the time of the census was nine days short of his tenth birthday and should have still been at school, was working as a domestic servant for Arthur S. Walker, a corn merchant, whose address was Bishopston Spa, Old Stratford. Although nearly ten surely his employment was unlawful, but it's doubtful whether many employers were sufficiently scrupulous to check on a child's date of birth, even if it was possible. Besides, William's age on the census form was actually recorded as nine so why wasn't Walker aware that he was in breach of the law? Was the family so poor that they were complicit

85

Above - FENNY COMPTON: The former Victoria Inn as a private dwelling. Pictured in 1978 it was later demolished..

Right and below - FENNY COMPTON: The route taken by James Jennings to and from the Victoria Inn: "On the night he was killed (1st July 1899) Grandfather walked over the bridge from right to left. He then came down the steps to get on to the path to walk home alongside the railway line. At this time there was another railway line (E&WJR) running under the left hand arch. It ran alongside the double track (GWR) as far as Fenny Compton Station, about a mile down from the picture and then branched off left to Stratford-upon-Avon." (FCJ, 1985.)

in hiring out their child's labour? Whatever the explanation, it looks as though some kids were still having a raw deal at the end of the nineteenth century.

 Sarah's health had begun to deteriorate, certainly by the latter half of the 1890s, so it's possible that might have had some bearing on William's situation. She had developed heart trouble and probably because of this, her husband, James, used to fetch a bottle of 'porter' for her from the local alehouse. Porter is a dark-coloured ale, brewed from charred or black malt, apparently resulting in a weak kind of stout. Presumably, like Guinness, it was 'good for you' and acted like a 'pick-me-up'. His kind deed was made all the more poignant by what was destined to take place – the event which initially sparked our interest in the family's history.

 The following is my interpretation of what happened, based largely on two contemporary newspaper accounts in the *Banbury Guardian* and the *Banbury Advertiser* (both dated Thursday, 6th July 1899), as well as information supplied by John Jennings. Whilst there are differences in some details recorded in the newspapers, there is no disagreement about the main event itself. During the evening of Saturday, 1st July 1899, James had set out along the railway track to the Victoria Inn to collect the said bottle of porter. The inn, on the Coventry to Banbury road, was near the Oxford canal and was known locally as the Tunnel Beerhouse. John Jennings explained that it had acquired this name 'because until the mid 1800s the Oxford canal ran through a tunnel at this location'. James's route took him along the section of the GWR and E&WJR lines where they ran parallel, towards the road bridge where he would have climbed up the bank beside the E&WJR track to access the road where the pub was situated.

 He left the inn at about 10pm, accompanied by John Hancox, whose wife was the innkeeper, as far as the road bridge. At this point the two men parted company, and James went back down the bank onto the railway line. It was a dark night for the time of year, being both wet and windy, so no doubt he was anxious to get home. But James was never to reach his house. When just two or three hundred yards away from it he was struck from behind by the local train, which was travelling from Blisworth to Stratford. He was killed instantly.

 From the evidence given at the inquest it is possible to work out the sequence of events leading up to the accident and why it had occurred. He was walking along the six-foot way of the E&WJR, which refers to the strip of land separating the E&WJR track from the down line of the GWR, when he became aware of the approach of a train on the latter. He would either have heard the train in the distance behind him and/or seen the GWR signals turn green. Wishing to move away from the oncoming train

before it passed him and, in the mistaken belief that the last local train that night had gone through, as it was due in at Fenny Compton at 9.59pm, he crossed over onto the E&WJR track – with catastrophic results. The train, which he thought had already arrived in Fenny Compton Station about the time he left the pub, was running 12 minutes late. He didn't hear it because it was slowing down as it neared the station and with steam shut off, it would have been running more quietly than at speed. The noise of the oncoming GWR train masked any sound coming from the local one.

 James would have been aware of the time as the E&WJR issued a fob watch to a foreman platelayer so that he could safeguard his gang when working on the line and alert them when a train was due – though not always successfully, as in his own case. (His was by no means an isolated incident for, according to Joby [ibid], platelayers accounted for a quarter of those killed on the railway in the early part of the twentieth century.) Although he couldn't read, he would have memorised the E&WJR timetable, the shortcomings of which were graphically illustrated when a train wasn't running to time. The locomotive struck him so forcibly, it was estimated that he was hurled some 30 yards along the track. He landed on his back, slightly askew, between the metals so that the train passed over him. Unfortunately, his left leg had come to rest on one rail whilst his right arm lay on the other, so both limbs were crushed, or even severed, by the train's wheels. The back of his head was badly damaged by the impact and from hitting the track. The description of his injuries in both newspapers make sickening reading, but this was normal for the time. In 'Easy Family History', David Annal says, '… there was nothing our Victorian ancestors liked more than reading about gruesome, horrific deaths at the breakfast table'. I feel sure the following account in the *Banbury Advertiser* would have satisfied their morbid fascination:

'The deceased's left foot and right hand were completely crushed, and the back of his head was smashed, the brains and a portion of the skull being found a few yards distant'.

 The sensitivities of the relatives were clearly not spared and nowadays it may seem crass and gratuitous to go to such lengths. (But are we in a position to criticise the Victorian obsession with blood and gore? Is it any more obnoxious than the current ridiculous cult of so-called 'celebrity' where every titillating detail of often talentless people's lives is subject to such scrutiny?) There were more touching revelations – for instance, the bottle of porter was *'smashed in a thousand pieces, but the cork that was in it was found on the line'* (*Banbury Guardian*). His cap and the basket in which he was carrying the bottle were also discovered at the scene.

FENNY COMPTON: The Oxford Canal, 1978.

Shortly after the accident, at about 10.15pm, James was found by Arthur Langford, a brickmaker, who was walking along the track from the station towards his home at Fenny Compton Tunnel. He returned to the station to raise the alarm and informed the signalman. The local constable was called out and, once he reached the scene, James's remains were placed on a platelayers' trolley and transported to the waiting room at the station. There the body was put into a coffin to await the inquest. This was held on the following Tuesday morning in the waiting room of the E&WJR, in the presence of the district coroner, Mr T. Christophers. Twelve jurors were sworn in, amongst them former colleagues of James. I recognised one surname – Allington – from my father's memoir. Was this a relative of Reuben, who later tracked down my grandfather in Somerset?

The first witness to be called was Charles Jennings, who stated that he had last seen his father alive at about midday on the day of the accident when *'he was then in his usual health'*. He confirmed that James had been a foreman platelayer, employed by the E&WJR and was 56 at the time of his death. (He wasn't, he was 60.) This must have been an extremely traumatic experience for Charles. My dad said he had identified the body and, as a result, hardly ever spoke of the accident. A common reaction in those

who witness horrific incidents as, for example, in wartime.

The next witness was John Hancox, who had left James at the railway bridge and was the last person known to have spoken to him. Hancox, a bricklayer employed by the Oxford Canal Company, had spent time with James that evening, in the pub run by his wife, and declared that he was sober when they parted. He watched him climb over the rails at the side of the bridge and make his way down onto the line. As he was walking down the bank, James had looked back and said, *'John, we shall be at work tomorrow ... We have an excursion coming down and shall have to walk the distance'.* As the following day was a Sunday, he was probably referring to a Sunday School outing, and, before it took place, James's section of the line would have to be checked but, alas, not by him.

Arthur Langford, who had discovered the body, was the next to give evidence, followed by the engine driver. The latter, whose name was Albert Silvester (according to the *Banbury Guardian* but William Silvester in the *Advertiser*), testified that the train was running late, arriving in Fenny Compton at 10.11pm instead of the scheduled time of 9.59pm. He had seen and felt nothing on the stretch of line where James was mown down, which he attributed to the darkness of that evening and to the fact that he was probably applying the brakes at that stage, thereby lessening the impact. He confirmed that a Great Western train had passed them, running on the parallel line and travelling in the same direction. The noise from that train would have prevented James from hearing the one which killed him. When news of the accident was relayed to the driver, he had examined the engine at Stratford and discovered *'marks on the air drum (sic), also on the fire box, which appeared to be blood'*.

Next up was PC Spraggett, who was stationed at Fenny Compton. He described what he had found at the scene, which he estimated was about 300 yards from the station. He had walked up the line a few yards, looking for evidence, and on finding *'the brains of the deceased and a portion of his skull'* was of the opinion that the victim had been *'struck and cut down by the buffer of the engine'*. He too added that James was a sober man.

When all the evidence had been gathered, the coroner summed up briefly, saying that undoubtedly James's attention had been diverted by the Great Western train so that, unaware of the local one, he had inadvertently stepped into its path. In a somewhat cavalier fashion, he added that men such as James were so accustomed to working on the railway that *'they were apt to get rather careless'*. The jury immediately returned a verdict of *'Accidental Death'*, and in a moving, but not uncommon, act of generosity, donated their fees to the widow. The next day, Wednesday, 5th July 1899, James's funeral took place in Fenny Compton Church and he was buried in the churchyard.

It is ironic that, if my great-grandfather had died in his bed, I would have known nothing of his character. From the newspaper accounts and an announcement in the parish magazine, I discovered that he was a decent, hard-working man, highly esteemed by all who knew him. The *Banbury Guardian* reported that he was a man of *'fine physique'* and *'was much respected in Fenny Compton ...'*. In the *Banbury Advertiser* it said, *'The deceased is spoken of as a steady, industrious man ...'*. The August 1899 edition of the parish magazine referred to *'a most lamentable accident on the East & West Junction Railway line, by which one of our neighbours met with his end very suddenly'*. It went on to say that he *'bore a high character'* and *'news of the accident caused great shock in the parish, and the deepest sympathy is felt by all for the widow and family'*.

How long after the accident and by whom Sarah was informed that she was a widow is not known. As it happened so close to home, it can't have been long before the dreadful news reached her. Fortunately, three of her sons were living close by – Charles might still have been at his parents' place – and it sounds as though there was a genuine desire in the community to help, as indicated by the jurors at the inquest giving her their fees. I don't know where she went to live as she would probably have had to move out of their cottage because it would be required for James's successor. That may sound heartless but the E&WJR was struggling financially throughout its entire existence. It would hardly have been in a position to accommodate its late employees' dependants.

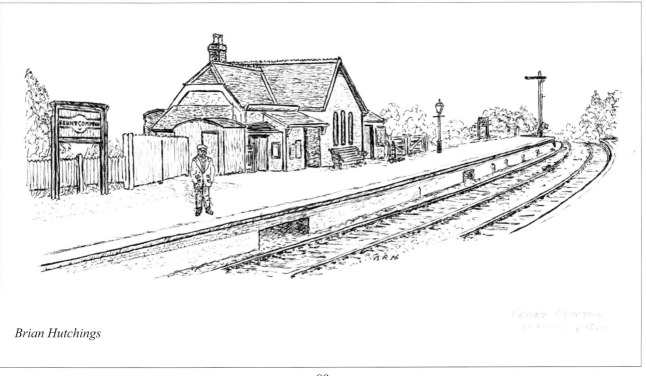

Brian Hutchings

FENNY COMPTON: The Parish Church, 1978.

Wherever she went, it wasn't for very long. Already in poor health, Sarah died on 3rd February 1900, seven months after James was killed. She was 58 years old, just 24 days short of her 59th birthday. Her death certificate gives her age as 57 (yet again incorrect) and the cause of death as *'Valvarum morbi (mitralis) 4 years'*. Jane Sheasby informed the registrar and was said to be present at the death. As Sarah's whereabouts are unknown at the time of her death, I can only guess at Jane's role. She lived close to Sarah's son, John, but I don't think there would have been room for his mother to live with his family. By 1901, Charles was living elsewhere in Fenny Compton and it's quite likely that his mother went with him. Perhaps it was here that Jane visited her, either acting out of friendship or employed, maybe by the parish, to nurse her.

My dad recalled that his father was convinced Sarah died of a broken heart, which sounded to me like something out of a romantic novel, without any basis in medical fact. However, this may not turn out to be as fanciful and far-fetched as I thought. There is a recognised condition called stress cardiomyopathy, commonly known as 'broken heart syndrome'. I encountered it in a delightful book, entitled 'A Shepherd's Life', by W.H. Hudson, which was first published in 1910 and set in rural Wiltshire. Hudson wrote of 'a strange phenomenon of death succeeding death in old married couples, one dying for no other reason than that the other had died'. He went on to say that it was quite common 'among persons of the labouring class in the rural districts'. The situation of James and Sarah accords quite well with this description, although Sarah already had an existing heart condition. The shock of the accident might well have precipitated her death; had James lived longer, she may well have too. They had been together for 40 years and he wasn't just her husband – he was the breadwinner and had taken care of her. Without his income, how would she have managed? She had died before the introduction of the state pension in 1908, and it's unlikely that she would have received an income from the railway company as James had not been killed whilst at work. Had that happened, she could have been given what Joby (ibid) describes as 'an ex-gratia payment from the railway and something from the provident fund if the deceased had been a member'.

The irony is that if James had been working, the accident might not have occurred. John Jennings explained, 'The E&WJR, although impoverished, did subscribe to the Standard Railway Clearing House Rules, one of which required any man walking the track at night to carry a lamp'. Had he complied, the train's crew would have been alerted to his presence on the line. The benefit of hindsight is a truly wonderful thing. The weather conspired against him too – 1st July is but a few days past the longest day of the year – as he could have reasonably expected to find it was still light when he left the inn.

The catastrophic consequences of James's death extended beyond the family in that all the people living at the Tunnel no longer had access to a supply of clean drinking water. They had been accustomed to drawing water from a spring beside the railway line, but the E&WJR had forbidden its continued use, understandably in the circumstances, as they wished to avoid further accidents. The only other available source of water was from the canal or the ponds, described in the parish magazine as *'wholly unfit for drinking or for use in cooking'* and which I reckon was more likely to cause a greater number of fatalities than collecting water from the spring. It went on to say that the District Council was arranging an alternative supply of pure water on a temporary basis but, in view of the hot weather, a permanent solution needed to be put in place quickly.

Even though I didn't know my great-grandparents, I felt saddened by the cruel hand fate had dealt them. Tragedy, in those days, was never far away from the doorstep of the poor, but there were others who suffered even greater loss.

Whilst scanning the contemporary newspapers for mention of the Jennings family, I came across a particularly haunting case, reported in the *Banbury Guardian* in 1900. Headlined *'A Warwickshire Tragedy'* it happened in the village of Rowington and involved the family of the village constable. One night, having completed the late shift, he arrived home at 2.30am, where he found his supper waiting for him as usual. After finishing the meal, he noticed that the door of the parlour, which led directly onto the road, was wide open. Very much alarmed, he dashed upstairs to find that his wife and their three children were missing, although he could tell that they had been in bed. Several neighbours were alerted and joined him in the search, but it wasn't until nearly 6am that the family was found. The mother had drowned her children and herself in the nearby canal. One of the neighbours retrieved the bodies, which were all together and still in their nightdresses. They were taken to the village inn, where the inquest was held the next day.

Over a century later, the account of the inquest is extremely harrowing to read. The poor mother had given birth just four months earlier so no doubt today would have been diagnosed with postnatal depression. Unfortunately, there was a history of mental illness in her family – her father and her sister had both been admitted to the asylum, and this had preyed on her mind. The local doctor testified that she had been *'morose and sleepless'* since the birth of her baby, and that her condition would have been exacerbated by the family history. She had told her mother that she was afraid *'the badness was coming out in the children'*. The contemporary view of insanity is revealed in the dialogue between the coroner and the doctor. In the latter's view, *'...insanity was apt to develop very suddenly, and an impulse might arise which it would be impossible to resist'*. The coroner asked, *'Is it a fact that a dream may be the cause of this sudden outbreak?'* The doctor replied, *'Yes, on a mind of that kind. It is very often after a sleep of "that sort" that all these suicides are committed'*.

It sounds as though these two professionals are really struggling to produce an explanation for the tragedy. Although their conclusion would be regarded as rather simplistic today, we can understand and share their turmoil in trying to explain the inexplicable. Worst of all was the effect that it had upon the father, whose anguish was palpable. So great was his distress that he could not continue giving his evidence and had to be helped from the room by his brother. It was generally agreed that they had been a devoted family – neighbours had noticed how the father would kiss his children when he came across them playing outside.

The coroner described the case as one of the most disturbing he had been called upon to investigate, saying that nothing could be more dreadful than what this young father had to endure. The verdict returned by the jury concerning the deaths of the three children sounds very harsh, being one of *'Wilful Murder'* by the mother, and in her case *'Suicide during temporary insanity'*. The coroner and the jurors were clearly moved by the father's plight, and the latter donated their fees to the police to start a fund for the bereaved man.

The untimely deaths of James and Sarah Jennings coincided more or less with the close of the nineteenth century, almost at the end of Queen Victoria's reign. Before we move to the next generation, there is a postscript to their story. In March 1978, my father wrote to the vicar of Fenny Compton to ask if he held any records which would assist in the search for more information about his grand parents. As he had received no reply after several months had passed, Dad decided the best course of action was to go to Fenny Compton and find out what we could. And so, on Sunday 20th August 1978, 79 years after the tragedy, we found ourselves looking at the place where it had happened. Although much had changed during that time and the old E&WJR track had been ripped up, it was still possible to make out where it had been, with the up and down lines of the GWR alongside it still intact. My father, Michael and I retraced James's footsteps from when he left the pub, along the road to where he went down the bank and onto the track. Michael and I walked a little way towards Fenny Compton Station so we had a good indication of where and how the accident happened. In case we were trespassing, we decided to leg it before we got caught, not out of concern that history may try to repeat itself.

From there, we visited Fenny Compton Church to see if we could find a gravestone in the churchyard for James and Sarah, but to no avail. In the village, Dad came across John Unitt, who lived at Rectory Cottage, and he was able to supply information about some of James's descendants who still lived there. Subsequently, he made enquiries about the location of James and Sarah's cottage, but too much time had elapsed for anyone to remember such an insignificant little dwelling, which had probably long since disappeared beneath an industrial estate. The house which the locals recalled was most likely the GWR stationmaster's house, too grand an affair for a humble platelayer.

Then, in October, my father received a reply from the vicar, with profuse apologies for the six-month delay. On consulting the church's burial register, he discovered the dates of James and Sarah's funerals and confirmed that they would have been buried in the churchyard. He too searched for their graves but was unable to find any trace of either. He added that the rector of the time had written a note beside the entry in the register about the nature of James's death. The moral of that story has to be, 'If you want a mention in dispatches, be sure to go out with a bang'.

PART 2 - A FAMILY HISTORY:

HENRY CHARLES JENNINGS

When Sarah Jennings died in February 1900, two of her sons, John and James, were married with families, whilst the two younger ones, Henry Charles and William, were still single. The final chapter of this saga features Henry Charles, my father's father, whose conduct gave the next generation such a shock that Dad's two brothers never spoke of it to their wives or children.

Following the visit to Fenny Compton in 1978, Dad was eager to find out more about his ancestry and asked Michael to continue the search. With attention now focused on the Somerset connection in order to trace the earlier generations, Michael and my dad delved into the records held by the County Record Office in Taunton. They came across lots of interesting material (some of which I duplicated later without realising it) and it was only a matter of time before my father began wondering about when and where his parents had married. By now we were into the early 1980s, before records were accessible 'on line', so it took much longer to seek out information. Luckily, Michael and Gill were living in London, and had relatively easy access to the records, then held at Aldwych, and to the newspaper library in Colindale where they had found the accounts of James Jennings's accident. It must have taken them hours of painstaking research, but try as they might, they were unable to trace any record of my grandparents' marriage. Unwilling to accept that there might have been something unorthodox going on, Dad put forward all sorts of possibilities to account for the missing document: perhaps it had been destroyed by fire or during the Blitz in World War II, or simply mislaid. Anything but the real reason, which was inconceivable to him: there *was* no marriage certificate because there was no marriage, at least between his parents. But worse was to follow as far as my father was concerned. It has to be remembered that what is acceptable behaviour today was then considered outrageous – cohabiting was a disgrace and illegitimacy was akin to having the plague.

Michael, despite the ominous signs, didn't give up and eventually his persistence paid off. He discovered that Charles Jennings had married on 6th June 1900 in the parish church at Farnborough, Warwickshire, not my grandmother but Alice Clara Dunn. My grandmother's name was Mabel March and she came from Bawdrip in Somerset. And the bad news didn't end there: Charles and Alice had a daughter. Aware of the distress that this was likely to cause my father, Gill and Michael came to tell him, face to face, what they had uncovered. To describe this information as a bombshell would be an understatement. Like many others of his generation, Dad viewed marriage as a life-long commitment – that's what you signed up for when you made your vows. To break them was regarded as little short of treachery. If only life were that straightforward.

I've been able to recount what followed, as the story unfolded, from my father's diaries and the communications which took place in the increasingly frantic quest to prove that the case against Charles Jennings was not as incriminating as it looked. The flurry of correspondence that followed began with another letter to the vicar of Fenny Compton, John Randall, the same incumbent as before, but who was actually about to move to another parish. He was unable to help as he said that all the registers from the relevant era were held by the County Record Office in Warwick. Dad immediately fired off a missive to the county archivist, in which he told of finding a marriage certificate for his father, Charles Jennings, who had married Alice Clara Dunn in Farnborough but was unable to find a record of his marriage to his mother. He made no mention of the daughter but said he was anxious to know if Charles and Alice had any children. I believe this omission shows the enormous difficulty he was experiencing in accepting that his father had compounded his 'treachery' by deserting not just his wife but his daughter too. He needed 'official' confirmation to convince him of the unpalatable truth, and that arrived promptly in the reply, dated 13th July 1984, from the archivist, Mr M.W. Farr. He had found an entry in the Farnborough register of the baptism of May, daughter of Charles and Alice Clara Jennings, which had taken place on 31st March 1901. The child had been born on 15th December 1900. Her father's trade was given as a *'dealer'*. Mr Farr discovered the marriage entry where Charles was again described as a dealer and the son of James Jennings, a platelayer on the railway, but came across nothing in the Farnborough records to show that Alice and/or May had died. There was now absolutely no

Opposite top - FARNBOROUGH: The Parish Church, 1985.
Opposite bottom - TAUNTON: Somerset Record Office (now located in Somerset Heritage Centre, Norton Fitzwarren), 1979.

doubt that this Charles Jennings was my father's father. Oh dear!

My poor dad was very shaken by all of this and, clinging to the fast-fading hope that there might be mitigating circumstances, he wrote to the archivist again. He asked if there could be a record of Alice's death in another parish as the family might have set up home in, say, Fenny Compton. Mr Farr, a very patient, understanding man, said that as the burial register for 1882 onwards was still in use at Fenny Compton, my father would have to contact the vicar there to see if Alice had died. In his opinion, speaking to local people in Farnborough or tracing members of the Dunn family would most likely yield results. He also suggested getting in touch with the Metropolitan Police to see if they could shed any light on the matter. There might be legal papers if Charles was separated or divorced which would probably be held at the Public Record Office (now the National Archives) in Kew. By the time Dad received this letter, dated 18th July 1984, Gill had been to Kew but could find no more than the dates on which Charles had joined and resigned. Not one to give up easily, my dad wrote again to the vicar of Fenny Compton on 30th July 1984, explaining he had been advised by the county archivist that, as the relevant burial register was still in use, he, the vicar, would be able to ascertain whether Alice Jennings had died in the parish.

This time back came a reply from the churchwarden, Peter Hughes, as the new vicar was not yet in post. The letter was dated 6th August, my father's birthday, but it didn't bring him any consolation, as there was no mention of Alice Clara in the burial register. There was an entry for May Jennings, who was buried there in April 1878, aged 16 months. Although the mystery surrounding Alice hadn't been resolved, it had answered another question, or so Dad believed. He was under the impression that his father was one of twins but that the other one, thought to have been a boy, had died at birth. Little May's details as stated would have made her the same age as Charles, but the year given for her death was inaccurate. Years later, I pursued this and discovered that she was the daughter of Charles's eldest brother, John. She was born on 29th November 1886 and had died in April 1888. I haven't found any indication that my grandfather was a twin – in fact, I think one like him was enough.

Undeterred, Dad pressed on, with a letter dated 25th August 1984 to John Unitt (whom he had met in Fenny Compton during our visit in 1978), in which he updated him on his progress, or lack of it. It now looked as though he was at last beginning to accept the situation but wishing that he'd not become involved, referring to 'my daughter and her husband who started this Family Tree business. (Regretfully?)'. I detect a note of irritation therein – it's entirely Gill and Michael's fault! The real purpose of this letter was to ask if Mrs Aldridge, keeper of the village

archives and mentioned previously by Mr Unitt, was still at her same address. Once he received confirmation that she was, Dad wrote to her, explaining that he was trying to trace his father's wife and daughter. He asked if she could suggest any other course of action. He received a speedy reply to say that Mrs Aldridge could find no mention of Alice or May in the Women's Institute histories of Fenny Compton. She was also aware that my father had been in touch with the churchwarden, Peter Hughes, who had asked James Jennings (Dad's cousin Jim) if he knew of Alice or May, but he did not. Fortunately, as she put it, 'a possible further line of enquiry came to mind' which had somehow led her to discover that Alice had been living in Farnborough and, even more tantalisingly, that May had married at Great Bourton in Oxfordshire. She went on to suggest that Dad write to the vicar there. Thanks to Mrs Aldridge's 'Eureka' moment, we were now hot on the trail of May, if not Alice Clara.

On 8th October 1984 a letter went off to the vicar of Great Bourton, but there was no reply. It was followed by another in November, reminding the vicar that my dad had enclosed a stamped, addressed envelope! For those growing weary of this convoluted tale, I'm pleased to say that the Rev Stephen Jones got in touch in January 1985, apologising for the delay but he had just taken over the parish. Nevertheless, he delivered the goods. He said that May was living in Little Bourton with her son, but he didn't know the correct postal address. However, he did provide the name and address of May's married daughter, who lived in Great Bourton. He must have been acquainted with them as he thought they would be prepared to answer Dad's queries. It's as well we did all this research at a time when people were willing to impart information, especially about others still living. I doubt whether many would be very keen nowadays and who can blame them? (I suppose much of it is currently available on the internet, which I find worrying.)

Meanwhile, my father had also contacted the Metropolitan Police to ask if they held any record to show my grandfather's marital status when he joined the force. He explained that Gill had visited Kew but was unable to find out any more than the dates of his service. His request was dealt with by a very helpful person in the archives department who actually asked for the relevant document to be returned to New Scotland Yard from Kew. He sent not only the details about Charles but also about William Jennings, who joined the same division on the same day. He asked if this might be my dad's uncle, which indeed it was. This was just one more example of the kindness my father encountered during his search. In his letter of appreciation, he confirmed that William was his father's brother. The final paragraph was very telling: 'When my daughter and son-in-law started this family tree business about five years ago, I did not expect them to find a skeleton in the cupboard, as they seemingly have done. However, until I establish whether Alice Clara was still alive in 1908 when I was born, I cannot reach any conclusion'. Oh yes, you can, Dad. Face it, will you – you are a bastard!

At the time, I did not realise the full extent of my father's hurt and disappointment – we used to take the mickey mercilessly but he took it all in good part. I think he was less concerned about the circumstances of his birth, that is, born out of wedlock, than about his father's desertion of his wife and daughter. It was as though Charles was diminished by it in my dad's eyes – he no longer seemed quite the decent, honourable man he had believed him to be. Gill asked him about a week before he died if he would rather not have known and he said yes. It had obviously troubled him to the end of his days, whereas the rest of us thought it mattered not one iota.

Although my father had gone to great lengths to establish May's whereabouts, it seemed that once it was within his grasp (the letter containing the information had arrived on 19th January 1985), he was confronted with a dilemma – do we proceed or do we stop here and now? The entries in his diary for 1985 show that he consulted his brothers, Cliff and Jim, and after much deliberation it was agreed that May would be contacted. Dad opted out of this one and handed over the job to Michael. It wasn't until 19th June that Michael rang to say that he had actually spoken to May on the phone, with the opening gambit, 'Does the name Henry Charles Jennings mean anything to you?' She said that it did, as he was her father. Michael then imparted the news that she had three half-brothers, which must have come as a hell of a shock to her – she was, after all, nearly 85 by now. He recalls that she sounded very interested in what he had to say during the phone call and so he followed it up with a letter. She sent him a photograph of her father and two of his brothers, taken when they were members of Fenny Compton football team, which she'd found in the *Banbury Guardian*, along with an invitation to visit her if he was ever in the area.

Eventually, my father and May met, on Sunday, 1st September 1985, at her home in Little Bourton. Five of us, my father and mother, Gill, Michael and I, descended on May, who was a widow, her son and daughter-in-law, her daughter and her husband and their daughter. Looking back, it must have been a surreal experience for all concerned, especially Dad and May, who were complete strangers, yet related. Clearly, they had a lot of information to exchange, and we spent a really pleasant afternoon with the family. It could have been an extremely awkward situation, but May was very gracious and not at all bitter towards her father. Dad did feel slightly uncomfortable and at times seemed as though he was apologising for their father's conduct. It had all

LITTLE BOURTON: *May and Fred meet for the first time on 1st September 1985.*

happened so long ago and May wasn't quite three when Charles had departed to join the Metropolitan Police. It's unlikely that she would have been able to remember him as I think her parents had not lived together for very long, more of which later.

When we left after several hours, I had the impression that it had been a very successful encounter, with both sides promising to keep in touch. Dad's low-key assessment of the meeting, which he recorded in his diary, is best expressed in his own words:

'Sunday, 1st September 1985 - we (including Gill and Michael) went to Fenny Compton.[1] Met May, her son and wife and her daughter and husband. May knew no more than she had already said, but she told of going to the RED LION pub at Fenny Compton each week until she was about 14 to pick up two shillings a week allowance from her father. Her mother evidently got nothing. Her mother went out into service until about

1. It was Little Bourton.

1911/12 and was at OLDHAM, Lancs. May was never told the reason for the break-up. Her daughter, Alice, thought it possible that Alice Clara was reluctant to follow father to London. She was strong willed'.

From reading that, I doubt whether anyone would guess that he was describing his first meeting with his half-sister when she was 84 and he was 77. They did write to each other occasionally and Dad, Mum and I visited on Sunday, 10th August 1986, when, once aging, we were made very welcome by May and her family. The contact continued right up until May's death on 7th October 1988, when she was nearly 88. Her daughter-in-law rang my father in the evening to say that May had got up out of her chair at 12.20pm and just dropped down dead – as Dad wrote in his diary that day, 'No notice, no suffering'. We were all genuinely sad to hear the news and, despite his diffidence about the whole affair, my father was very pleased to have met her. It's a pity she didn't meet her other two half-brothers, but that would have meant revealing 'the skeleton in the cupboard' to their families and they clearly wanted to avoid that. I am sure Dad would not have enlightened us, had we not been involved from the beginning, and I recall him asking us not to mention it to anyone. But, as Gill remarked, it was much too good a story to keep to ourselves, so we didn't.

To return to the cause of the 'scandal', Charles Jennings, who had experienced rather an incident-packed start to the new century. First of all, he'd had to deal with the deaths of both his parents so close together, which must have been traumatic for him and his brothers. By looking at the dates available to me, I have tried to add some detail to his story. Following his mother's death in February 1900, Charles had married Alice Clara Dunn in June of that year. May was born in December of the same year so, yes, he was keeping up the family tradition of marrying to the sound of gunshot rather than that of wedding bells. 'Try before you buy' was the well-established motto of the Jennings menfolk. The dates show that the baby was probably conceived in March, which would mean that Alice was about three months pregnant when they married, and thus the likely reason for the marriage. Their marriage certificate shows that, at the time, Charles was living in Fenny Compton and Alice in Farnborough. He was 23, a bachelor and a dealer by trade. She was 25 and a spinster with no occupation recorded for her. If this were a Barbara Cartland novel, I'd be claiming that Charles, after losing his mother, sought solace in the arms of an older woman, or similar bunkum.

May's birth certificate states that she was born in Fenny Compton so that must have been where her parents set up home after their marriage. Alice registered the birth on 24th January 1901 and was said to be still living in Fenny Compton. Charles had apparently packed in the dealing to become a journeyman baker. So far, then, it appears they were living together as a family.

Shortly afterwards, I believe the marriage had started to go wrong. On the day of the census, 31st March 1901, May was baptised in Farnborough, and she and her mother were staying at the home of Alice's father and stepmother at The Mutton in Farnborough. But Charlie-boy, now shown to be a dealer in the baptismal record, was still

BAWDRIP: King's Sedgemoor Drain alongside which stood the house where Mabel was born, 1988.

BAWDRIP: Trish standing on the site – in the early 1980s the house was demolished, 1988.

Bottom - *BAWDRIP: Was this Mabel's birthplace? 1975.*

POWIS CASTLE: Mabel was in service here, date unknown.

living in Fenny Compton. Does this signal the break-up? He had taken a lodger, Charles Green, a single man aged 20, who worked as a railway platelayer. On seeing this, my first thought was, 'Blimey, is this the original rent-boy?' but, knowing my grandfather's reputation for being 'fond of the women', I soon discounted that idea. On the census return, he was described as the head of the family, married, aged 24, with yet another occupation, that of 'carrier', working on his 'own account at home'. So, in the space of ten years, he'd been an agricultural labourer, a dealer, a carrier, a journeyman baker and goodness knows what else that wasn't recorded, plus those yet to come.[2] This bloke had more jobs in his lifetime than I've had hot dinners, a regular 'jack of all trades and master of none'. Dad used to say that his father was hopelessly impractical – he couldn't knock a nail in straight and his attempt at learning to drive was disastrous. It has to be said that he was a good athlete, wrote poetry and was a skilled card player, none of which provided a regular income. Had Alice become so weary of his inability to stick at one job that she dumped him and went back to her father? Whatever the truth of the matter, it seems certain that Charles and Alice had married for reasons of conformity and respectability and not because it was a love match.

The next confirmed date in Charles's chequered career was that on which he joined the Metropolitan Police, 16th November 1903. As we have seen, May's daughter thought that Alice Clara had refused to accompany her husband to London, as she was said to be a quiet, country girl, unused to city life. My feeling is that this is not the likely reason and that the marriage had failed long before. Apparently, May said she could remember a man coming to their house in Farnborough whom she later assumed to have been her father, indicating that she had never really known him. Instead, his youngest brother, William, made the journey with him and they both joined the force on the same day. Both were assigned to the Whitehall, or 'A', division, Charles as PC 285 and William as PC 304. Their warrant numbers were 90282 and 90283 respectively. Charles's previous occupation was described as 'a carrier – in business for himself', whilst William had been a platelayer on the E & W J Railway, like his father before him. With Alice and May tucked safely away in Farnborough, Charles embarked on a new career which, as usual, wasn't destined to last very long.

It was during his time in the Metropolitan Police that he met Mabel March, but could I establish where, when and how? This was not going to be easy as my grandparents were determined to cover their tracks, which they managed very successfully. A fitting starting point seemed to be to look into Mabel's story, to see if there were any clues as to how their paths had ultimately crossed. She was born on 28th April 1881 in the village of Bawdrip in Somerset, the daughter of Elizabeth (nee West, also born in Bawdrip on 15th March 1850) and Frank March, who was a farm labourer. Mabel had four sisters, Mary (known as Polly), Rose, Isabella Sophia (Soph) and Elsie, and three brothers, Thomas (Tom), Frederick and Henry J (Jack), who are mentioned in my father's memoir. She left home when she was 12 years old – the age when I was in the first form at grammar school – and started work as a scullery maid, the most menial position in a household. It's believed that she worked in Clifton (the posh part of Bristol), Powis Castle in Wales and Lowther Castle. The latter was the stately pile belonging to the Earl of Lonsdale, who also owned property in London and Barleythorpe Hall in Rutland. It is at the latter that Mabel can be found on the 1901 census, having risen to the dizzy height of kitchen maid at the age of 19. On that census return, I noticed that there were no offspring listed for the Earl and Countess, but there was a huge retinue of servants living under their roof, plus many more obviously connected to the estate, such as grooms, gardeners and gamekeepers. Mabel's employer, then, was a seriously wealthy geezer who, I thought, required further investigation. Was he a decent employer or just another greedy bastard who exploited the lower class?

Hugh Cecil Lowther was born on 25th January 1857, the son of the third earl and the brother of the fourth, whom he succeeded in 1882 as the fifth Earl of Lonsdale. With a pedigree as long as mine is short, what a colourful character he turned out to be. His interests and achievements were so many and varied, it's just not possible to cover them all and besides it's well documented elsewhere (e.g. see 'Oxford Dictionary of National Biography'). On his marriage to Lady Grace Cecilie Gordon in 1878, he had taken up residence near Oakham in Rutland, where both indulged their passion for hunting. There were no children from this union, as his wife had not only lost a baby following a hunting accident, but became a semi-invalid and unable to have any more kids. That must have been particularly difficult to bear, as her husband certainly didn't curtail his activities.

On the death of his brother, Hugh became one of the country's wealthiest men. He owned around 175,000 acres of land and his properties where Mabel is known to have worked included Lowther Castle in Cumberland, Barleythorpe Hall and Numbers 14 and 15 Carlton House Terrace in London, which had actually been knocked into one. He entertained many distinguished visitors, among them 'Kaiser Bill' (the German Emperor Wilhelm II), who was at Lowther Castle to shoot grouse in 1895 and again

---

2. A noted in Fred's memoir, my grandfather used to go to London during the First World War to buy old street horses at auction which he then sold locally. So we can add 'horse trader' to the list, but I suppose it shows how enterprising Charles was.

LOWTHER CASTLE, 1975.

in 1902. The kings of both Portugal and Italy were also known to have visited. I don't suppose Mabel saw any of them, though she might have had the dubious honour of cleaning their boots, the lazy sods. Such friendships would have been brought to an abrupt end at the outbreak of World War I – if only they'd stuck to shooting grouse.

Apart from being the master of several hunts at various times, most notably the Quorn and the Cottesmore, Lonsdale's sporting connections must have been legendary. He owned racehorses and was frequently seen at race meetings; once an amateur boxer, he became heavily involved in the sport and was the instigator of its most prestigious prize, the Lonsdale belt (which even I, no boxing fan, have heard of); he also took part in greyhound racing and yacht racing. As if that wasn't enough, he became president of the Arsenal Football Club, first president of the Automobile Association and, in 1907, the first president of the International Horse Show at Olympia. He was known as 'the yellow earl' because of the colour of his carriages and livery, not as a reference to a lack of bravery. I wondered if my father was aware that Mabel's former employer had been the AA's president, the organisation Dad joined on leaving Shapwick. Michael confirmed that he had been as he had lent him a book about the earl. Incidentally, the colour yellow became associated with the AA in recognition of its first president, which it has retained to the present day.

Lonsdale's reputation was tarnished in 1885, when he became embroiled in an extra-marital affair and was cited in a divorce petition. He had become infatuated with Violet Cameron to such an extent that he took her, and the opera company he was financing for her, to New York to escape the ensuing scandal. That didn't have the desired effect, so they returned to London, where Violet gave birth to a daughter. Hardly the most effective way to quell the gossip and so, in 1888, Lonsdale departed to colder climes - in an attempt to cool his ardour? He travelled to the Arctic Circle, enduring hardship unknown to many of his class. Philanderer now turned explorer made him a hero on his return, and he donated his impressive collection of artefacts from his travels to the British Museum.

Variously described as generous, energetic, genial, extravagant and friendly, he sounds to have been something of an exhibitionist, or a 'poseur', as we say now. You may not have been impressed by his exploits, but you certainly couldn't have ignored them. As a result of his profligacy, financial problems ensued, resulting in the sale of some of his properties. Barleythorpe Hall was sold in 1928, only to be destroyed by fire in 1934. In 1957, one hundred years after Lonsdale's birth, the roof of Lowther Castle was removed, presumably to avoid crippling death duties and the high cost of maintaining such a building. He didn't live to see this, another likely consequence of his extravagance, as he died on 13th April 1944. His wife, with whom he had been reconciled, predeceased him in 1941. Both were buried at Lowther Castle, which is now being rescued from further decay by a charitable trust to the tune of some nine million pounds.

Whilst I definitely do not regret the passing of the master/ servant era, I do lament the destruction of so many stately homes which contained much of the nation's history, now sadly lost to future generations.

Most important of all for me was that the earl sounds to have been a benign employer. He actually had a special train transport his household between residences, instructing his valet to tip the stationmasters concerned with a £5 note apiece. Judging by these travel arrangements, it looks as though Mabel would have joined his staff initially in London, at Carlton House Terrace, making the journeys to the other properties along with the rest of the servants. It is not known how long she was in service with the Lonsdales, but my father thought she had entered their employment during the mid to late 1890s. He attempted to find out by contacting the County Record Office for Cumbria, but no records of the Lonsdale family after 1875 were held there. He was advised to write directly to the estate manager at Lowther, but drew a blank there as well because staff wage books were not kept before 1905.

Clearly, this line of enquiry wasn't going anywhere to establish where and when my grandparents first met. I thought that perhaps Mabel's older sister, Rose, might have provided the link as she was already living in London, having married George Willcocks (also from Somerset) in 1902. He too was in the Metropolitan Police, so had he introduced Charles to his wife's sister? As the two men were not working in the same division – George was in 'N' – it appears unlikely. Carlton House Terrace, though, lay within the Whitehall ('A') division, so Mabel and Charles were working in the same locality. My dad and Michael had speculated about how they might have become acquainted and concluded that Charles could have nipped into the kitchen at Carlton House Terrace for a quick cuppa while pounding his beat. No doubt he would have recognised the kitchen maid's Somerset accent as similar to that of his parents, for it was very pronounced. I noticed it as a child and asked why Grandma said 'vish, vire and vowls' instead of 'fish, fire and fowls'. I can't recall the reply but remember that she was amused at the time, though she it's possible she thought, 'This one's going to be trouble'.

Assuming that their work had brought them into contact, there is no way of establishing exactly when, but it had to be some time in 1907 at the latest. All I had to work on now was my father's birth certificate, two photographs and several indisputable dates. What follows, then, is largely what I have been able to piece together from this evidence. At this stage, I was beset by questions galore, many of which are never going to be answered. For instance, when was Mabel made aware that Charles was already married: before or after she became pregnant? Had they already made a commitment to each other or was it a hasty decision brought on by the pregnancy? Either

way, they needed to make plans for the future together. There were several considerations to be taken into account, which may seem bizarre nowadays. Mabel's reputation was at stake for, as an unmarried mother, she would have been shunned and without a means of support if Charles had deserted her. Any unfortunate finding herself in such a situation was confronted with a stark set of choices: get rid of the child somehow, face life in the workhouse or, even more drastically, end up in the river. Was it really necessary to go to such lengths? It is difficult to understand, over a hundred years later, just how terrifying it was for a single girl who found herself pregnant. I wondered whether I might have been exaggerating the consequences until I came across the horrendous practice of 'baby farming', which was certainly not uncommon during the Victorian period. It provided a way out of the intolerable situation faced by an unmarried mother, unable to support her child. Isn't it amazing how there is always some unscrupulous individual waiting in the shadows to cash in, quite literally, on the misfortunes of others? A baby farmer would place an advertisement in a newspaper, offering to 'foster' or 'adopt' unwanted babies, for a given sum of money. This was, of course, a subtle way of contacting single mothers who were desperate and couldn't afford, financially or morally, to care for their offspring. Some chose to turn to the baby farmer in the mistaken belief that it was the least worst option. If a child was to be 'fostered', payments would have to be made at regular intervals, whilst a one-off sum would secure its 'adoption'. The outcome was always the same, whatever the agreement, as it was a massive scam. A 'fostered' baby was slowly poisoned or starved to death in order to extract maximum payment from the mother. Sickly babies weren't rejected but were 'adopted', as they were good value since they perished quickly. The mother would be too ashamed to admit that she had farmed out her illegitimate baby and so the death often went unreported. The tiny, emaciated bodies were just dumped in the river or somewhere out of sight.

Some baby farmers were caught and prosecuted, resulting in notorious trials, like that of Amelia Dyer in London, as late as 1896, a mere 12 years before my dad was born. It had taken a long time before the practice was outlawed and probably even longer before it finally ceased. But the degradation and humiliation heaped on an unwed mother didn't stop, and continued well into the twentieth century. In the 1950s, I remember the scathing remarks aimed at girls unlucky enough to get 'caught out' and who were referred to as hussies, sluts, tarts, or worse. Little wonder, then, that Charlie and Mabel wanted to take their secret to the grave.

Although Mabel would have borne the brunt of people's scorn, Charles's career prospects wouldn't have been enhanced if he was found to be living a double life – in

The 'bride and groom' and the 'wedding party'? Venue unknown, circa 1907.

fact, he would very probably have been dismissed. It was to the advantage of them both to present a respectable image to the world and there was only one way to do that: claim to have married. Easy enough to carry out: buy a wedding ring and fix a date when they could say they had tied the knot quietly or in secret – no banns were necessary if you bought a licence. All could be done and dusted in a very short space of time. Perhaps Charles relied on his brother William to corroborate their story and agree that he had acted as a 'witness' to add credibility. This raises the question of how many others were privy to the secret. The fewer who knew, the less likely it was to be divulged. Had Mabel taken her sister, Rose, into her confidence? Although she was staying with her when Dad was born, it doesn't prove that Rose knew the whole story. If she did, it was little short of miraculous that she kept it quiet, as she wasn't known for her tact and diplomacy.

The two photographs I mentioned earlier, which were kindly sent to me by my cousin, Janet Hubert, could contain some valuable clues. One shows my grandparents dressed very smartly, possibly in their 'wedding' outfits, with Mabel holding a posy and Charles sporting a floral buttonhole. It seems to have been taken in a back garden, but of whose house? The other photo, probably at the front of the same property, could include guests invited to celebrate the occasion as my grandparents were still wearing the same attire. In an attempt to discover the location, I sent the photos to Rose Willcocks's granddaughter, Mary, who lives in London. Unfortunately, she was unable to identify any of the participants and ruled out her grandparents' place in Oldfield Road. Another possibility was the home of William Jennings, as he had already married Lily Annie on 17th August 1907. The census of 1911 shows them living at 46 Russell Gardens, Stangate Street, Lambeth, so was this the setting for an alleged 'wedding breakfast'? As we have seen from my father's description of that address, his uncle's flat was part of a six-storey block, so it wasn't there. However, it seems that William and Lily had previously lived elsewhere as their son, Albert, slightly younger than my dad, was born in 1909 in Upminster, Essex, and thus after the event in the photograph. Perhaps the family had taken up residence in Russell Gardens soon after Albert's birth. So much time has passed that it's unlikely that anyone (other than Charles and Mabel) in the group photo will ever be identified.

Above - BAWDRIP: "Bawdrip Church interior: me standing by the font in which I was christened by Rev Townsend, 18th October 1908, 80 years ago". FCJ.

Right - BAWDRIP: St Michael and All Angels' Church, 1988.

The photos could provide an indication of the time of year when they were taken. I suspect it was during the spring as there are leaves on the tree in the background, with the shrub directly behind the couple not yet in leaf. The hanging basket at the front door shows a few flowers, with the windows above opened a little. One or two of the women seem to be quite warmly clad and my grandfather looks to be wearing a fairly substantial waistcoat (perhaps more to do with custom than the weather) beneath his jacket. If it was late March/early April, when Mabel was three or four months pregnant, it would tie in well with the length of the 'marriage' which Charles later recorded as three years on the 1911 census. It was one thing to have to admit to a hasty marriage, but quite another to have been openly living 'in sin', for which they would have been pilloried. It's impossible to tell if Mabel and Charles did live together in London, or exactly when Mabel had left the Lonsdales' employment. Charles continued in the police force and, by the time of Dad's birth, Mabel was at 2 Oldfield Road, Stoke Newington, with Rose and George. She was still there when she registered the birth on 31st August, but the remainder of their time in London is destined to remain shrouded in mystery.

Almost two months after Dad's birth were to pass before Charles resigned from the Metropolitan Police, on 2nd October 1908. Was this to give them time to contemplate their next move? They were undoubtedly faced with a dilemma: stay in London, where he had a good job with a pension, but risk being found out with all the consequent shame and scandal, or make a fresh start elsewhere. They opted to move away to where they hoped their secret would be safer. Both had connections with Somerset so there wouldn't have been any disagreement about that destination.

The next definite date of their whereabouts, now with little Fred in tow, is 18th October 1908, when he was baptised in Bawdrip Church, in my grandmother's home parish. Presumably, they stayed at the home of Mabel's parents until they moved to the Albion Inn at Ashcott, just a few miles from Bawdrip. Once again, Philip Hocking at the Record Office came to my aid and discovered documents relating to the family's time at the Albion. As Charles's occupation at the time of my dad's baptism was recorded as 'ex-policeman', he had not yet become the pub's landlord. This took place between October 1908 and 21st January 1909, the latter being the earliest

BRIDGWATER: This is the earliest known photo of Fred (1911). On the envelope in which it was stored, someone – most likely Aunt Soph – had written, "Aunt Elsie took Fred on the back of her cycle into Bridgwater from Ashcott to have this taken". A framed enlargement of a similar photo, taken on the same occasion (but, thankfully, minus the girly hat) used to hang on the wall in my grandparents' sitting room at the New Inn. As children, we were highly amused by his outfit and used to refer to the time when 'Daddy was a little girl'.

mention of his tenancy. According to the 'Valuation List for the Parish of Ashcott', [3] the Albion Inn, along with an orchard, owned by the brewery, Starkey Knight & Co of Bridgwater, was occupied by H.C. Jennings. The Inland Revenue Domesday Survey of 1910 [4] reveals that the property also included shops, as well as the pub and orchard, but as Dad never made reference to the former, I have no idea what they comprised. There is also an interesting entry in Kelly's Directory for 1910:

'Ashcott: Henry Charles Jennings, good accommodation for commercial travellers; dinners and teas provided;

parties catered for; every convenience. Albion commercial inn'.

This amused me as the description hardly equates with that given by my father – more of a 'spit and sawdust' outfit from what he said. One thing, the food would have been good as Mabel was an excellent cook. Her jugged hare (ugh!) was reputed to be second to none. It's easy to see who would have been doing most of the work – and with two small kids to look after. The place was much bigger than I had realised - according to the 1911 census, there were ten rooms, excluding *'scullery, landing, lobby, closet, bathroom ...'.*

So far so good, then, till along came that bloody intrusive census of 2nd April, with the inquisitive state asking questions I expect my grandparents would have preferred not to answer. But Grandad had his own back and spun `em quite a yarn. I wonder if he thought, as I often do when form filling, 'I'll teach the buggers a lesson, if they insist on poking their long noses into my business'. He was far more creative than I'd ever dare to be and turned in a right work of fiction. It was the first occasion that householders filled in the census form themselves, and even though the schedule declared, *'The returns are not to be used for proof of age, as in connection with Old Age Pensions* [5] *or for any other purpose than the preparation of Statistical Tables'*, Charlie was taking no chances. His responses reveal that he wanted to avoid any mention of Fenny Compton and London, and to that end stated that his birthplace was Stogumber in Somerset. Yes, he was married, but for rather longer than the three years he entered on the form. To be fair, it did require *'Completed years the present Marriage has lasted'* so what else was he to do? There were two children *'still living'* from this 'marriage', but only Clifford Albion Jennings, aged 11 months, was listed. My dad was missing, so what had his parents done with him? As might be expected under the circumstances, they had bundled Fred off to stay with his grandparents in Bawdrip, thereby avoiding any reference to his birthplace, Stoke Newington in London. [His grandfather, Frank March, had stated it accurately, but he had first of all entered Dad as a *'Visitor'*, then crossed it out in favour of *'Granson'* (sic).] Well done, Charlie, I bet that put the snoopers off the scent – if there were any. How he must have chuckled as he signed the declaration at the end that *'this Schedule is correctly filled up to the best of my knowledge and belief'*. Oh, sure it is! There was one visitor entered on the census form and that was Elsie March, my grandmother's 17 year old sister, who had taken Fred to Bridgwater on her bicycle to have his photograph taken. If that had taken place during her stay at the Albion, then he would have been not quite three years old.

3. Ref: D/R/bw 15/3/2.
4. Ref: DD/IR/T 2/2.
5. Introduced in 1908.

Three photos of Henry Charles and Mabel, on the farm and probably at the New Inn, dates unknown.

I noticed in the space designated to be completed by the enumerator that he was asked to certify, *'After making the necessary enquiries I have completed all entries on the Schedule which appeared to be defective, and have corrected such as appeared to be erroneous'.* That's what you think, mate. I'd like to see how Charles completed the next two census returns for 1921 and 1931 (there wasn't one in 1941 because of World War II). I hope he had a good memory or kept a record of his fairytale, otherwise he could have given the game away.

It is evident from my father's account that my

grandparents didn't stay anywhere for very long. After seven or so years at the Albion, they were on the move again, this time to the neighbouring village of Shapwick, where they lived in three different properties. Charles was either a naturally 'restless kinda guy' or felt the need to keep on the move to avoid his past catching up with him, which indeed it did with the unexpected appearance of Reuben Allington from Fenny Compton. He must have given Charlie the surprise of his life when he crawled out of the straw in one of the outhouses on Bowerings Farm. That was bound to have caused some consternation – how had Reuben managed to trace him? Poor chap probably

SOUTH PETHERTON: The Wheatsheaf (the former New Inn but now closed down), 1979.

SOUTH PETHERTON: Henry Charles Jennings, landlord of the New Inn.

SOUTH PETHERTON: Henry Charles (in the overall, khaki-coloured of course) with some of his cronies outside the New Inn. The soldier on the left suggests this was taken sometime during World War II.

wished he hadn't bothered, arriving with only one eye then leaving minus his hand. My father said he wasn't told how Allington had caught up with his dad – easy to guess why not, isn't it? Perhaps the 70 quid from the insurance had helped to buy his silence, as he couldn't have gone blabbing all round the village.

In 1934, Mabel and Charles made their final move together to the New Inn in South Petherton. He was the landlord there until his death on 29th December 1949, at the age of 73. Thereafter my grandmother kept it going until the late 1950s, when she fell ill with stomach cancer. Eventually, she went back to Bowerings Farm in Shapwick to stay with her son, Clifford, and his wife, who had taken over the farm, and she died there on 12th July 1960. I hope that my grandparents' life together had not been blighted by concerns about being 'found out', for theirs seems to have been a genuine love-match. Mabel was distraught when Charlie died, declaring him to be the only man she'd ever truly loved. (She had been engaged

to someone else before she met my grandfather.) I recall Dad saying that, at the funeral, she had to be restrained from chucking herself into the grave.

The day Mabel had walked into his life was a lucky one for Charles, as she was a decent, kind, hard-working woman. She must have trusted him implicitly – had he not stuck by her, she would have been ruined. Fortunately, he did stay the course although there were rumours that he might have occasionally 'played away from home'. One really surprising aspect is how their secret had remained just that for so many years. Too much time has elapsed to determine exactly who did know, and the only certainties are Charles's brothers and, of course, Reuben Allington. After my dad's death, I asked his cousin, Elsie (Aunt Soph's only child, also born at the Albion), if she was aware that my grandparents weren't married. She grinned, and would only say that another cousin, Harry, (the son of Mabel's sister, Elsie) had claimed there was a possibility Mabel and Charlie hadn't been able to marry. If some of the March family had been in the know, it's even more remarkable that they had remained tight-lipped for so long.

My grandparents' case was by no means exceptional – couples were forced to go to great lengths to conceal an illicit union because of the opprobrium it attracted. From what I can remember of them, it's hard to imagine Mabel and Charles in this position. My memories of my grandfather, who died when I was eight, are of a rather stern, forbidding man. He was the stereotypical Victorian, who believed that 'children should be seen and not heard'. At mealtimes, he used to say, 'Everytime you speak, you miss a mouthful'. Work that one out if you can – I'm still mystified by it. I recall him wearing a knee-length, khaki-coloured overall, though I don't know why as by all accounts he spent more time dodging work than doing it. Perhaps it was to prevent his clothes from getting covered in snuff, the use of which I regarded, even when a child, as a filthy habit. He'd take a pinch of it from his snuffbox, place it on the back of his hand and snort it up one nostril, then the other. It was revolting and I wasn't keen on kissing him because some clung to his moustache. His preferred occupation was to sit in the pub's lounge bar, playing cribbage, or 'crib', with some of his cronies. He must have torn himself away occasionally to serve other customers, as he didn't allow women behind the bar, except when it suited him. Whilst many people of my generation can speak of their grandfathers as war heroes, it rather looks as though mine was more of a draft dodger. I may be doing him an injustice, as it's possible that he was suffering from an undiagnosed dislocated hip, a legacy of his sporting activities. He was a member of Banbury Harriers Athletic Club, and his achievements in both 100-yard and 220-yard distances were quite impressive, resulting in some worthwhile prizes, among them a couple of mantel clocks, a pair of silver vases and cutlery. He must have been dedicated, as he entered two races a couple of days before his marriage. Michael found an account of the Banbury Athletic Sports and Cycle Parade in the *Banbury Advertiser* of Thursday, 7th June 1900. In the 100-yard race, Charles ran in the second heat and was going well, only to fall when close to the tape. Ouch, the humiliation! He tried his luck in the 220-yard race, and was again entered in the second heat. This time, he finished in second place, having run ahead and *looked like winning easily'*, but was pipped at the post. He was beaten in the final and didn't figure in the prizes. Perhaps he was a little apprehensive about his forthcoming nuptials, which had put him off his stride. A pity, as the first prize for the 100-yard race was a sterling silver Queen Anne teapot, which would have been a useful wedding gift.

After joining the Metropolitan Police, Charles became a member of Highgate Harriers and, once again, Michael discovered a piece about the Chiswick Annual Sports in the *Chiswick Times*, dated Friday, 19th August 1904. Grandfather had obviously improved his technique for, in the 100-yard open handicap, he won with a ten-yard mark. This sounds to have been a pretty big occasion:

'Among the attractions in the grounds were roundabouts and swings, Aunt Sallies, cocoanut (sic) *shies, etc, while the band of the T division Metropolitan Police performed the ……. excellent selection of music'.*

The day concluded with an *'al fresco concert'*, and *'dancing to the strains of the band'* went on until nearly 11 o'clock, when the patrons all went home. They sure knew how to enjoy themselves in those days and, no doubt, without the need to smash up everything in sight.

So far I've presented a rather negative, facetious picture of my grandfather, and now it's time to redress the balance because he was not a bad man. There are some positive aspects to his story, which are worthy of note. As we have seen in my dad's account, his father took an active part in village life, and it must have required some initiative and enthusiasm to organise local events. He became a churchwarden, a parish councillor and sub-agent to the Conservative Association, and seems to have been well liked and respected. All that could have changed in an instant if his 'secret' had been discovered, quite unfairly in my opinion, as a man's character should not be wholly judged by one mistake. Besides, when Alice Clara became pregnant, Charles had taken the honourable step of marrying her. He could so easily have pushed off and left her in the lurch, claiming that the child wasn't his. He also continued to support his daughter financially, unlike his grandfather before him, though his generosity wasn't extended to his wife.

Among the first generation of the family to have definitely received an education, he would have realised how handicapped his parents were by their illiteracy. I view the move to join the Metropolitan Police as a means of self-improvement rather than to avoid his family responsibilities. His police service was relatively short-lived as fate intervened and he met Mabel. A similar pattern emerged in Shapwick where, attempting to improve the family's standard of living and its social status, he progressed from running a couple of smallholding-type establishments to the much larger farm. His reason for vacating the Albion wasn't very patriotic – in order to evade being called-up – but entirely understandable at his age and with his disability.

Unquestionably, Charles and Mabel were good parents to their three sons and, in the case of Dad and Cliff, endeavoured to obtain the best education available to them at the time. It was very unfortunate that the funds ran out before either of them had really completed their schooling. My grandparents were so proud when my father succeeded in joining Gloucestershire Constabulary as a letter from the vicar's wife, Mrs Seamer, demonstrates. I came across it whilst sorting through Dad's effects. Dated 27 April 1931, she wrote to congratulate him on fulfilling his ambition to become a policeman, at a time when employment was extremely hard to find. How did she know his parents' reaction? Irony of ironies, Charles had arrived that day to collect the census form. Was his slogan, 'Falsification of census returns our speciality'? I gained another little snippet of information from this letter as Mrs Seamer went on to say, 'Your mother has been most kindly lending us a hand by making us most excellent pies once or twice a week and that has been a help to me'. Just a bit more evidence showing how my grandparents were involved in village life.

If the world could be divided into romantics and pragmatists, then I see my grandfather as one of the former and Dad as one of the latter. Grandfather's life seems to been quite adventurous – he swapped jobs so frequently that eking out a living must have been precarious at times, though the family appears to have been better off than many of their village contemporaries. In contrast, Dad served 31 years in the police force, which then offered stable, secure employment. It provided accommodation and a good pension, which he continued to draw for 41 years, much to his delight. Neither set the world alight, but each had aspirations for their children, that they should have better lives than their own, and recognised the value of good schooling. I have grown to admire my grandfather, who overcame adversity and surely made amends for his misdemeanour. Furthermore, I am sincerely grateful to him and my grandmother for producing the finest father anyone could ever wish for. So, here's to you, Charlie and Mabel!

Before concluding this chapter featuring my grandparents, there was one task left to do, and that was to find out what had happened to Charles's three brothers. John, the eldest, of whose existence I knew nothing until I started my research, remained in Fenny Compton, working for the E&W J Railway as a platelayer, like his father. I managed to trace five children for John and his wife Elizabeth (known as Betsy). Sadly, two of them died in infancy – I've already mentioned May, who died in 1888, and Fred died on 19th February 1892, aged just 12 months, from inflammation of the lungs. John and Betsy could have had more children as, at the time of the 1901 census, she would have been about 40. She died before her time on 18th February 1914, aged 53, in Fenny Compton. John continued working as a 'ganger' until 3rd September 1921, when he retired at the age of 60, and he died in Fenny Compton on 4th March 1930, aged 69.

James and his wife, Catherine Ann, produced at least ten children, but sadly Catherine died in childbirth on 12th September 1914, aged only 41, just a few months after John was widowed. James retired from his job as a railway platelayer on 5th January 1938, when he was 65, and died in 1952, aged 79, in Willesdon, Middlesex, where he had been staying with one of his daughters. He was the only one of my grandfather's brothers whom I knew, from his visits to the New Inn at South Petherton.

William, the youngest, retired from the Metropolitan Police on 6th June 1927, and then went to live at the Mill House in Shapwick and worked on the farm. I don't know how long that arrangement lasted, but presumably when my grandparents left Bowerings Farm, William and his wife returned to Braintree in Essex, where she came from, and he died there in 1942. His son, Albert, emigrated to Canada, where he died on 15th December 1983.

At the seaside: from left to right: Trish, Hilda and brothers James and Henry Charles

PART 2 - A FAMILY HISTORY:
THE END OF THE LINE

We have almost come full circle. This book opened with the account written by my father of his early life and will end with him, as he was the last of the male line in our branch of the family. I am attempting to complete the circle by picking up the tale where Dad left off.

Having put a stone, allegedly, through a shop window in Wincanton, he was transferred by the Automobile Association to Aston Cross, near Tewkesbury in Gloucestershire. (I don't know if there was a connection between that incident and his move - the AA might have wanted him out of the way, sharpish! I find it impossible to imagine my reliable, responsible dad 'burning rubber' on his motorbike so that it chucked up a stone – it's totally absurd and completely out of character.) He was in lodgings with someone who was related to, or knew, the chief constable, or his assistant, of that county. It was suggested that he should apply to join this force, having been turned down by the Metropolitan Police and Somerset Constabulary, on what now appear to be spurious grounds, but it shows how difficult it was to get a

job then. Their loss, however, was Gloucestershire's gain as he was accepted and became PC 49 on 7th September 1931. For those not old enough to remember, PC 49 was the character who featured in the radio series during the late 1940s. My dad was also told many times how much he resembled another fictional bobby, Dixon of Dock Green, played by the actor Jack Warner in the BBC series of the same name

.

Dad was stationed in Gloucester, and it was there that he met my mother, Hilda, in 1932. He was on point duty on Gloucester Cross, near where Mum worked, and was introduced to her by one of his colleagues. They married in St Paul's Church on 16th February 1935, six days after my mum's 21st birthday, because Dad said he wasn't about to marry a minor. It wasn't a 'shotgun' wedding – it appears that they broke the mould as I wasn't born until 1941, when World War II was well underway. During the war, Dad was posted to the police headquarters at Lansdown in Cheltenham, and Gill was born in the Imperial Nursing Home there in 1948. Towards the end of 1949, we were on the move again when my father

Left - PC 49, with regulation greatcoat, 1931/32.

Right - ASTON CROSS: Fred the AA patrolman, outside the Queen's Head Inn, 1931.

Fred at HQ on joining Gloucestershire Constabulary, 1931

became the sergeant in charge of Staple Hill Police Station, which was then the southern-most point of Gloucestershire Constabulary. He remained there for the rest of his service.

It is disappointing that he didn't include his time in the police force in his memoir as it would have made interesting reading. The anecdotes he used to relate were many and varied, some amusing and others tragic. For instance, he told of the time when, as a young constable, the police were called to assist in recovering a body from the railway track because someone had committed suicide. Dad and his colleagues placed the corpse on a wheeled stretcher as it had to be removed from the station along a very narrow path. The path was bordered by metal railings and would have been wide enough to accommodate the trolley had it not been for the victim's arm, which was sticking out at a right angle. Unfortunately, rigor mortis had set in so the arm could not be moved and struck each of the metal posts with an eerie clunk, clunk, clunk as the procession made its way along the path. At this, there was much black humour in evidence, which shouldn't be seen as contempt for the deceased but as a necessary mechanism for coping with a macabre situation.

But some incidents were too dreadful for that. The crash of the Britannia aircraft whilst making a test flight was

such a case. It happened in Downend, near Bristol, on 6th November 1957, and thanks to the skill and heroism of the pilot, who narrowly missed a row of houses, much greater loss of life was averted. All those on board were killed as the plane came down in a nearby wooded area. The gruesome task of retrieving the body parts and wreckage was down to the emergency services, including my father. The remains were placed in dustbins to remove them from the scene, which could only be described as complete carnage. My mother said that it was the one occasion that my dad was unable to eat his dinner as a result of doing his job, so badly traumatised were he and his colleagues.

The policeman's lot wasn't only about death and destruction and there were lighter, more pleasant aspects to it, including policing the Badminton Horse Trials and Cheltenham Races. It was at the latter that I took the opportunity to meet Dad whilst I was at St Mary's College in Cheltenham. I found him chatting to a weirdly dressed individual, who turned out to be Prince Monolulu, the racing tipster. I remember very little of the encounter except that, as we shook hands, the self-styled 'prince' passed some comment like, 'Woman, what fingernails you have!' I admit that they were extremely long, and hideous, but I don't think they warranted the attention his attire did. He was sporting a very colourful outfit with a headdress made from ostrich feathers, making sure that you weren't going to miss him in a crowd. A prince he was not, his real name was Peter Carl Mackay and it seems that he was born on the Caribbean Island of St Croix in 1881. This made him a contemporary of my grandmother, Mabel March, as she was born in the same year. Although she may never have come across him, there is a strong possibility that he would have been known to her former employer, the Earl of Lonsdale, one of the 'horsy' set. As the most famous black man in this country at the time, surely Monolulu's celebrated cry as a tipster, 'I gotta horse!' would have been familiar to the earl. The 'prince's' life story was every bit as flamboyant and adventurous as Lonsdale's – he had been shanghaied and interned in a German prisoner-of-war camp during World War I – and it is recorded in his memoir, appropriately entitled 'I gotta horse!'

Recently, I met the person I was in lodgings with when we started at St Mary's College over 50 years ago. We hadn't seen each other since our college days and, much to my surprise she mentioned our day at the races, which must have been in 1961. She recalled meeting Prince Monolulu and that he had noticed my fingernails, thereby confirming it was not a figment of my imagination. If only I had realised that I was in the presence of such greatness, I would have requested his autograph. At the time of our meeting, he must have been 80 years old, and we were fortunate to have seen him as he died four years later on 14th February 1965. The current age sadly lacks eccentrics like him – he had entertained the crowd and added such colour to the racing scene. All you see now are women in outrageous hats and ridiculous footwear, each trying to outdo the other.

A couple of incidents, which particularly amused my dad, concerned Queen Mary while she was staying at Badminton House. Two plain-clothes officers were patrolling the grounds when they came across her, ripping ivy off the walls of the house. Her hatred of the climber was legendary as it damaged the stonework, so she persuaded the two coppers to join in – not exactly police work but how could they refuse? I'm not sure if the following happened on the same occasion, but one officer's hat was taken by the wind and deposited on the lake, well out of reach. Unbeknown to the policeman, his plight had been observed by Queen Mary, who presented him later with a new trilby hat. No doubt he passed on that tale, and maybe the hat as well, to his grandchildren.

After 31 years in the force, my father retired on 31st October 1962, and on his certificate of service his conduct was described as 'exemplary' (which is exactly what I would have expected) written in the chief constable's own hand. That probably didn't impress Dad greatly as he considered Mr Gaskain to be an arrogant twerp and, in a moment of disrespect, referred to him as 'Gasmain'. The very smart barometer given to him by his colleagues of 'B' division was a much more welcome reminder of his days as a policeman. He went on to manage a small business for his cousin Elsie's husband, until that had run its course, and then he concentrated on his garden – and writing his memoir. When he was 81, he had a prostate operation, which was followed by some serious complications. We were warned that he was very ill and unlikely to survive as he was suffering from septicaemia and tuberculosis in the spine, which may have lain dormant for years (the legacy of drinking unpasteurised milk on the farm?). But Dad had other ideas and proved to be something of a medical miracle. He succeeded in getting back on his feet with tremendous input from the physiotherapists at Frenchay Hospital, and then attended the local day centre. Always keen to embark upon some new challenge, he decided to try his hand at weaving. It proved to be an excellent choice and, although he needed help in selecting colours (he was mildly colour-blind in that he couldn't distinguish between green and brown), the finished products were entirely of his making. Several pieces of his work were exhibited locally and he won a few prizes. His enthusiasm was such that he made himself several hand-weaving frames so that he could indulge his new interest at home.

Fred on a Brough Superior motor patrol combination, rear of Gloucester Central Patrol Station, about 1933.

PS 49, Staple Hill, 1952.

My father had always been very resourceful, the origins of which no doubt went back to his youth. Gill said that his ingenuity knew no bounds and he could fashion a wheelbarrow out of a washing machine – or was it the other way around? Unfortunately, one of his 'good ideas' backfired and could have had fatal consequences, certainly for me. It happened in about 1948, when many houses were not fitted with electric wall sockets. My mum used to do the ironing in the living room, as there was no space in the kitchen (more of a scullery), which housed a full-sized bath. (I used to say that we kept the coal in the bath, which greatly annoyed my mother because she thought it made us sound like slum dwellers or 'back streeters'.) To accommodate her iron, Dad replaced the light bulb fitting with a double bayonet socket, enabling an extension lead to be fixed to the wall at a height my mum could reach. Now she could use her iron and have the ceiling light on at the same time. It was also handy for testing light bulbs, which I'd seen my parents do. One evening, whilst Mum was bathing Gill in front of the fire, I strategically placed a chair so that I could reach the extra socket and inserted a bulb. Unluckily for me, it was a torch bulb. There followed an almighty bang, the room was plunged into darkness and I was flung from the chair. Apparently I had a very fortunate escape, with only blackened fingernails and a shattered torch bulb to show for my foolhardiness. Poor old Gill narrowly missed being drowned in the bath

as our mother must have been very startled, believing that blackouts had finished at the end of World War II. Once she realised what had happened and my father, armed with a torch, had repaired the fuse, their attention turned to the cause of the near catastrophe. I was not popular. Secretly though, I'll bet they were relieved that the outcome hadn't been a lot more serious. From that moment on, I developed a healthy respect for electricity, as it is potentially lethal. In fact, if it were discovered today, it would most likely be banned by the Health and Safety Executive, an organisation which may be necessary (but I doubt it) and certainly is extremely irksome.

This episode might make my mother and father look like irresponsible parents, but that is so far from the truth. When we were growing up, we would have claimed that they were over-protective. Although the world in many ways was a safer place for children, my police officer dad was only too aware of the existence of paedophiles. They just weren't dignified then with such a posh-sounding label, which tends to obscure the true nature of their vile trade. They were generally referred to as 'dirty old men', not politically correct (another irritating modern phenomenon perhaps more fittingly described as 'pretentious claptrap', 'preposterous codswallop' or just 'plain crap') but well deserved and appropriate. It's only later in life you realise that parents were acting out of

BADMINTON HOUSE, 1979.

concern for your welfare and not from a desire to spoil your fun, even though they often did.

To return to the state of my father's failing health: in 1999 he was struck down by a stroke which affected his ability to swallow. Miraculously, he recovered again, but it marked the beginning of the end. Having survived many serious illnesses against all expectations, my seemingly indestructible dad finally succumbed on 1st November 2003, not in his own bed but in Frenchay Hospital which he said in his later years had become his second home. He had achieved his ambition to live in two centuries, but had become very tired and 'ready to hand in his musket', as he described it. Undoubtedly the worst moment of my life, it was, paradoxically, something of a relief to witness his life ebbing away peacefully and undramatically, as he had suffered so much. Throughout his twilight years he had borne the deterioration in his health with his customary stoicism, and was unfailingly polite and grateful to those charged with his care. The doctors and nurses did everything possible to make him comfortable but, in the end, it was time to let go. It was hard to accept that, this time, he wasn't going to stage a comeback, but we received lots of sympathy cards, in which some people took the opportunity to say that it had been a privilege to have known him. One card, from my dad's assistant physiotherapist in Frenchay Hospital, simply said, 'Goodbye to a legend', which sums it up more succinctly than I ever could.

At 95, he had outlived many of his contemporaries, including his two brothers, but is still remembered by many people, not least of all for his philosophical sayings. He'd often quote Sammy Ayres's expression, 'God doesn't pay his debts with money', so hold that thought when a brick falls on your foot. There were too many others to mention them all, but my favourites include, 'You can tell what God thinks of money by those he gives it to' (can't you just - bankers perhaps?), 'You catch more flies with honey than you do with vinegar' and 'It's better to be 20 minutes late in this life than 20 years too early in the next'. The latter was frequently directed at me when I was cursing some dawdling or inconsiderate driver.

What kind of a man, and father, was Frederick Charles Jennings? The adjectives used to describe his grandfather, James, spring to mind: steady, industrious, well-respected, of fine physique. To these we can add good-humoured, self-deprecating, genuinely interested in what others had to say, someone who did not seek to impress and, of course, the world's greatest hoarder. (Unlike me, he always knew where everything was stored. Years later, I actually came across that infamous torch bulb, or what was left of it, but I have no idea where it is now. I wondered why on earth Dad had kept it but still couldn't bring myself to sling it out.) Make no mistake, though, he wasn't a pushover and, if provoked, his displeasure was apparent and often accompanied by a hefty dose of sarcasm. He bore no malice and quickly recovered his amiable disposition. An utterly devoted father who, I am quite sure, would have given his life for us and never once let us down, even though he claimed he could have given me away 'with a packet of tea' when, as a toddler, I had a temper tantrum on a bus. Despite that remark, he was, quite simply, the best – a delightful man indeed and one I am so pleased and proud to call my father.

I miss him to this day – my dad who had taught me to read, to knit (a scarf which had, unintentionally, more holes than a string vest), to ride a bicycle (purchased from the police lost property sale for ten shillings. I couldn't reach the pedals so Dad fitted them with wooden blocks), and to drive … well, no, not quite. His patience had worn a little thin by then. Gill and I remember his comment when I was practising driving his car on a disused airfield. Unfortunately, I'd driven into a large pothole, at which he wasn't amused and remarked, somewhat pompously I thought, 'A good driver would have missed that'. I was crushed, but that's how it was – losing his approval was far more effective than all the slaps dished out by my mother.

There is a postscript to this chapter, too. Although my father stated in his will that he wished to be cremated, he didn't specify what was to happen to his ashes. We couldn't decide what to do, so the container languished in my airing cupboard where, after my mother's death three years later, it was joined by her ashes. I began to amass quite a collection as not long afterwards my two cats died and ended up in there as well. It was time for some action, as my parents needed a final resting place together. What better spot could there be than in the village Dad always regarded as 'home'? Gill and I discussed it and she suggested we wait until his 100th birthday on 6th August 2008. On that day, with our cousins, Janet and Ann, we gathered at our grandparents' graveside in St Mary's Churchyard in Shapwick, and watched as the oak caskets containing Mum's and Dad's ashes were laid to rest alongside those of my father's brother, Cliff, and his wife. The ashes of the two cats also went in, Mabel (named after my grandmother as they shared the same birthday) with Mum, and Spike (after Milligan) with Dad. As it now says on the commemorative stone plaque above the grave, they are 'Together Forever'. I'm certain my father would have approved of our decision and, as for my mother, she said she wanted to be with 'Freddie', so she got her wish. When my turn comes, it's where I want to be, so I hope someone will take note of that and act on it!

As I looked around the graveyard, I was reminded of how death is the great leveller for, situated not far away from our modest plot, is the vault of the Strangways family. More ostentatious and impressive it may be, but there is no private entrance for the haughty lady of the manor now. She died, aged 95, on 3rd October 1949, just a couple of months before my grandfather, and now lies alongside some of her former tenants, all her equals in death. My dad's diagnosis of her 'problem' with the lower orders? A chronic case of 'ingrown virginity'. Only he could get away with such a 'bloke-ish' remark in a household of women. I also came across the grave of that old philosopher, Sammy Ayres, who died on 16th October 1961 at the age of 69, and his son, Herbert Joseph, who went on to become the mayor of Bridgwater four times. How proud his dad would have been of that achievement.

Like most English villages, Shapwick has grown but not beyond recognition. I can picture my dad and his brother as they roamed around the country lanes and raced across the fields, airguns in hand and bagging whatever was stupid enough to cross their path. Wearing hobnail boots and those massive caps, plonked on their heads like giant cowpats, they must have presented a fearsome spectacle. They certainly gave Grandmother March a fright as they announced their arrival with an airgun pellet through her window. She probably thought that the Wild West had come to Bawdrip. But their days of rampaging through the countryside are long gone, and they are reunited in the tranquillity of an English village churchyard, far from the turmoil and turbulence of the modern world. May all those who lie beneath that small patch of land with the Jennings name on it be resting in peace.

Dad was still weaving at the ripe old age of 90!

PART 2 - A FAMILY HISTORY:

AND FINALLY...

Having reached the end of this fairly light-hearted jaunt through the family's history – with due deference, I trust, to the very real suffering of some of those involved – it seems appropriate to outline briefly how and where I obtained the information, as it may be of some use to others intent on a similar mission.

First, a word of warning: researching the ancestry can soon become addictive and take over your life. It is compelling, intriguing and, at times, frustrating and disappointing – but never boring. I compare it to working on a vast jigsaw puzzle which has pieces missing and no picture to act as a guide. Even though it's going to be incomplete, you hope that you'll get enough to give a good indication of what took place. My intention from the outset was not to build up a family tree, going back in time as far as the records would allow, but to find as much detail as possible about the relevant individuals so that they became more than just a set of names and dates. I had a head start as I tried to put 'some flesh on the bones' of the ancestors (perhaps not the best choice of words in the circumstances) because Michael and my dad had done much of the groundwork for me to build on. They had acquired most of the relevant and available birth, marriage and death certificates which contain a lot of valuable material. Once the civil registration system had been introduced in England and Wales in 1837, the task thereafter of tracking down individuals became easier, although success isn't necessarily guaranteed as we have found out.

The census returns (available for 1841 to 1911) provided a useful starting-point to begin my search, even though they don't always contain wholly accurate information, deliberately or otherwise (Grandfather, please note). For this reason, it was essential to try to verify what I discovered by tracing as many other original documents as possible, and for those I turned to the county record offices. I opted to employ the services of their researchers as they are so skilled in accessing the records. I am greatly indebted to Philip Hocking at the Somerset Record Office (now in Somerset Heritage Centre at Norton Fitzwarren), who turned up some very interesting material, including the settlement papers relating to James and Harriet Jennings. I made several visits to the record office in Taunton but there is much that I could have easily overlooked without Philip's assistance. (Even so, despite our best efforts, details of my great-great-grandparents' deaths have eluded us.)

Although there is a great deal of material available on the internet, I preferred using good, old-fashioned books; many have been written on the subject of genealogy, and some provide historical background as well as ways of tracking down your ancestors. The most comprehensive I found was 'Ancestral Trails' by Mark Herber, which covers just about everything that you need to know. Bibliographies are a valuable source of further reading. Without exception, all the librarians I contacted were extremely helpful (including those at the Library Information Service) in giving advice and sending me copies of useful material. The staff at the Somerset Studies Library solved a couple of mysteries for me and suggested further avenues to explore when I thought I'd reached a dead end.

Contemporary newspapers are another useful resource, especially in cases of notoriety or tragedy – I was fortunate that some of my forebears had warranted the attention of the authorities and the press. I contacted the paper which had covered the inquest into my great-grandfather's accidental death to find out if there were any of his descendants still living in the Fenny Compton area. I am grateful to the editor who agreed to publish my letter appealing for anyone who could help to get in touch. It resulted in a phone call from Ruth Williams, who is the granddaughter of my grandfather's brother, James, and she advised me to speak to her sister, Sonia Smith. Sonia produced photographs and much relevant information about Fenny Compton and Northend, where she still lives and where, in the summer of 2009, Gill, Michael and I had the pleasure of meeting her, her husband and Ruth. Neither side knew of the other's existence prior to my letter to the *Banbury Guardian*, but still we found plenty to discuss.

Finding hitherto unknown, living relatives was an enjoyable spin-off of my research as it's a pleasant change from just dealing with those long gone. Another contact came about as Gill looked in the visitors' book in the church in Bicknoller. There she found an entry made by Stephen Jennings, who had included his address – just a few miles from where I live. Luckily, his phone number was in the local directory and we have met a couple of times to exchange information. He is descended from my great-great-grandfather's brother, Thomas, and so is Kathleen Mullins whom I found mentioned amongst the subscribers in 'The Book of Crowcombe, Bicknoller and Sampford Brett' by Maurice and Joyce Chidgey.

Kathleen lives in the village of South Petherton where my grandparents kept the New Inn. I also managed to re-establish contact with Bridget Humphrey, the granddaughter of Dad's half-sister, May, and she was able to tell me a bit about her great-grandmother, Alice Clara, who outlived Charlie and Mabel.

I pursued many false trails, but occasionally even these had a positive outcome. For instance, I had noticed some photographs in a book entitled 'A History of the Stratford-upon-Avon & Midland Junction Railway' by R.C. Riley and Bill Simpson, which were taken from the collection of J.R. Jennings. Convinced that he must be a descendant of James Jennings, I tried to contact him through the publishers of the book, Lamplight Publications. I never did manage to find the latter but even better, through a somewhat circuitous route, I reached Kevin Robertson, who not only agreed to produce this book but provided me with endless suggestions of who might be able to assist with my research. It was through Kevin that I got to talk to Bill Simpson and also to Barry Hoper of the Transport Treasury. Thanks to Barry I was finally able to establish contact with John Jennings who isn't related but is the archivist for the SMJR (which merged with the E&WJR). I am extremely grateful to John as he went to great lengths to establish the site of the frame house occupied by James and Sarah Jennings. He also gave me a valuable insight into the working conditions of nineteenth-century railway workers. This run-of-the-mill tale of an ordinary family led me in some quite unexpected directions, and no individual or organisation was immune from my persistence if I thought they could be of help in my quest. My sincere apologies go to all those I harassed but without their input the story would have been much less complete. I reiterate my thanks to the many friendly, helpful people, often total strangers, for their patience and tolerance, who were certainly under no obligation to give of their time so generously.

I suppose I could be accused of an act of betrayal for divulging family secrets, but my defence is that I have not revealed anything that cannot be found on public record, available to anyone who cares to look. All those who may have by affected by it, including my father, are beyond being hurt. Those so-called transgressions – moral rather than criminal – are commonplace today and would pass unnoticed. It's only in the context of the age that they were considered scandalous and shocking. How times change – and not necessarily for the better. Life is certainly easier and more comfortable nowadays but I suspect we are not really any happier or more contented than previous generations. The universal, twin evils of greed and 'man's inhumanity to man' (and to animals) are still very much in evidence, and we are treated to illustrations of both on a daily basis. Through the wizardry of modern technology, world events, good and bad, are relentlessly beamed into our homes but the improvements in global communication have not yet led to greater understanding between nations as the Victorians had hoped.

When you consider the perils confronting our planet today – global warming, its natural resources under ever-increasing strain as the population tops seven billion, the banking system in meltdown, and so on – it's difficult to maintain a sense of optimism about its future. So far, we have been able to rely on man's ingenuity to build on the legacy of our forebears to keep us ahead of the game. But are we now reaching the stage where we are so far removed from our roots that we are in danger of destroying that which sustains us? My father certainly thought so. During one of the massive falls on the stock market, brokers on the floors of the stock exchanges around the world were filmed wringing their hands and wailing as they agonised over the crash. While pandemonium reigned, my father's comment was that they would have been better off out in the fields, hoeing turnips. A seemingly facile or trite remark perhaps, given the gravity of the situation, but I think I'm beginning to understand what he meant. It seems a fitting end to this tale, to have given him the last word – almost – with one of his typically astute observations.

Meanwhile, there is no going back, even if we wanted to, so in the immortal words of this nation's great orator, Sir Winston Churchill, we have no choice but to 'keep buggering on'. And that is a sentiment which my dad would have wholeheartedly endorsed.

BIBLIOGRAPHY and SOURCES

ADOLPH, Anthony 'Tracing your Family History' (Collins, 2007)

ANNAL, David 'Easy Family History' (The National Archives, 2005)

CHIDGEY, Maurice & Joyce 'The Book of Stogumber, Monksilver, Nettlecombe & Elworthy' (Halsgrove, 2003)

CHIDGEY, Maurice & Joyce 'The Book of Crowcombe, Bicknoller & Sampford Brett' (Halsgrove, 2005)

COLE, Anne 'An Introduction to Poor Law Documents before 1834' (Federation of Family History Societies, 1993)

COLEBY, Ian 'The Minehead Branch 1848-1971' (Lightmoor Press, 2006)

HART-DAVIS, Adam 'What the Victorians Did for Us' (Headline Book Publishing, 2001)

HERBER, Mark 'Ancestral Trails' (Sutton Publishing Limited, 2005)

HEY, David 'The Oxford Guide to Family History' (Oxford University Press, 1998)

JOBY, R.S. 'The Railwaymen' (David & Charles Limited, 1984)

JORDAN, Arthur 'The Stratford-upon-Avon & Midland Junction Railway' (Oxford Publishing Company, 1982)

MANSFIELD, Paul 'A Bicknoller Diary 1860-1868' (2008) and 'A Bicknoller Diary 1868-1910' (2009)

OAKLEY, Mike 'Somerset Railway Stations' (The Dovecote Press, 2002)

RICHARDS, Tom 'Was Your Grandfather a Railwayman?' (Federation of Family History Societies, 3rd edition, 1995)

RILEY, R.C. and SIMPSON, Bill 'A History of the Stratford-upon-Avon & Midland Junction Railway' (Lamplight Publications, 2007)

THOMSON, David 'England in the Nineteenth Century' (Penguin Books Ltd, 1950)

The Victoria History of the Counties of England: A History of Somerset, Vols II and V (The University of London Institute of Historical Research)

ARTICLES OBTAINED FROM THE INTERNET

BLACKETT-ORD, Mark 'Lowther, Hugh Cecil, fifth earl of Lonsdale [1857 – 1944] (Oxford Dictionary of National Biography, Oxford University Press, online edn, Jan 2011)

'LONSDALE', Who Was Who, online edn, Oxford University Press, Dec 2007

McCONNELL, Anita 'Mackay, Peter Carl [1881 – 1965] (Oxford Dictionary of National Biography, online edn, May 2010)

HALLER, Dorothy L. 'Bastardy and Baby Farming in Victorian England'

HANCOCK, Ralph - Wikipedia